LEBRON

I HOPE YOU ENJOY
READING THIS WITH YOUR
KIDS AS MUCH AS I
ENJOYED WRITING IT FOR
MY KIDS. THANKS FOR
REDEFINING THE GAME
AND WHAT IT MEANS TO
BE AN ATHLETE. YOU, LIKE
KOBE, ARE EVERYTHING THIS
BOOK IS ABOUT.

CHRIS

BRAIN ENGINEERING FOR ATHLETES,
STUDENTS AND TEACHERS

B.E.A.S.T.

THINKING

A young athlete's guide to managing stress, improving
performance and developing a success mindset.

CHRIS McCAIN and TUCK TAYLOR

ISBN: 978-1-6847-1111-6 (sc)
ISBN: 978-1-6847-1113-0 (hc)
ISBN: 978-1-6847-1112-3 (e)

Library of Congress Control Number: 2019915167

Lulu Publishing Services rev. date: 02/06/2020

This book is dedicated first and foremost to my two sons, Hayden and Hudson. Never could I have imagined having two sons who are as smart, loving, generous, and motivated as the two of you. You have made my life better from the moments you arrived. It is for you that I strive every day to learn, grow, and be the "beast" that I can be.

This book would not be possible if it weren't for my wife, Stacy, who has been a significant asset in helping raise two unique children who one day will go on to enjoy tremendous success in their lives. There are many wild and crazy things that eminate from my mind, and she has not dismissed or challenged most of them. Thank you to my family for giving me the freedom to be creative, proactive, and most of all daring with the way I live.

To the parents who entrust me with physical, mental, and emotional development of your kids: this book is dedicated to you and your kids. I hope that through the work we do together, all of them find incredible success in their lives.

—Chris McCain

***

Ten years ago, the idea of writing a book would have never been anything I would have dreamed of accomplishing. As I started my journey in the health and wellness industry, I always felt my job was to coach, train, and teach. My constant search for knowledge and how to help people find the best in themselves physically and mentally has gotten me to where I am today. This book has given me an opportunity to share some of my own ideas and experiences, and hopefully it will inspire and motivate others to examine their lives through a different lens.

This book is dedicated to all my family, friends, and associates who took time to share their wisdom and knowledge with me throughout my journey to define my own path and purpose for my life.

In the process of completing this book, I became a father. My son, Teddy, has inspired me and given me a new passion for life, and I look forward to sharing this book with him one day.

—Tuck Taylor

***

In memory of Kobe Bryant. Kobe was a tremendous inspiration for this book. The Mamba Mentality embodies everything that is growth mindset and grit. Kobe forever changed the standard for establishing a path to greatness by admitting to and focusing on the importance of passion, perseverance, determination and the will of the human mind.

CONTENTS

ACKNOWLEDGMENTS

TO ALL OF the people who have influenced this book: you are deserving of tremendous praise and gratitude. To my peers who help me think in a manner that is positive, creative, and influential on a scale I could never have imagined. To my friends and fellow dads and coaches whom I have played basketball with and coached with or against: thank you for helping me continue to learn the game of basketball. These men include Teddy Dupay, Rich Hollenberg, Dave Finley, Colin Shaw, Speedy Smith, Doug Scull, Jim Carr, Ronnie Taylor, Jordan Fair, Marreese Speights, Greg Popovich, and Steve Kerr. Okay, maybe the last two are a stretch, but if they end up reading it, then they will remember me. Each of you has helped me over the years, and your knowledge, conversations, and ideas are critical to the development of this book.

To the core group of kids whom I have coached through the years, including Hayden, Hudson, Calvin, Kamrin, Kaleb, Jeremiah, Jason, Nick, Max, Deon, and Rivers, you kids have forever changed my love for the game of basketball, and your future is a big reason for me writing this book. I wish you all incredible success and hope that I will continue to be a part of your personal growth.

I cannot forget a special thanks to Walt Rivenbark. Walt, you struck the match that reignited my desire to learn and grow, which in turn has become a raging forest fire to not only continue learning but share this information through writing and speaking.

To all of the individuals who have volunteered their time to read small portions and iterations of this book: your opinions, edits, and ideas have been instrumental in the final product. As parents, fellow coaches, and players, your experience has made this book an invaluable tool for kids and parents.

Finally, a special acknowledgment to my coauthor, Tuck Taylor. Your knowledge and open-mindedness toward human growth, development, and success are exceeded only by the energy and enthusiasm with which you share them with the world. It didn't take long for me to know that a synergy would arise that would allow us to bring something new and powerful to the world. Double tap, Tuck Taylor! You are the original BEAST.

—Chris McCain

***

My life's experiences, both good and bad, were always made more bearable with the love and support of my family. My father, mother, and sister have always been there for me. Whether it was attending my basketball games, helping finance my California internship, or helping me realize my dream of owning my own gym, my family has always been my private troop of cheerleaders.

As a young entrepreneur, I thought a mentor or business coach would be essential to my success. I found a phenomenal mentor in Mr. Terry Ogborn. Terry spent countless hours with me and helped me understand the keys to running a successful business. I credit him with introducing me to the world of personal and professional development. Some of the principles I learned from him can be found in this book.

Senecha Lewis, aka PK, a friend and colleague whom I have known most of my life, came to be an integral part of my life when he joined my gym in search of a transformation to a healthier lifestyle and much-desired weight loss. PK allowed me to mentor him and share with him the tools and knowledge needed to become successful in his journey to better health. Although he came to me for training and coaching, it was he who became the teacher and I the student. He taught me more about drive, dedication, and commitment than any of my prior experiences. Thank you, PK, for inspiring not just me but others as well. Thank you for your loyalty and support as I chase my dream one person at a time.

A large thanks to the other staff of Beast Athletics: Kendra, Joe and Raymond. Your commitment to the success of our business afforded me the time to make this book become a reality.

Thank you to my Goddaughter, Lai Lani. As my one-person, middle-school focus group, your feedback and questions during the process helped me ensure that the message was on target for today's young athletes. Thank you for helping me more fully understand the mindset of a young athlete.

Thanks to Mike Pine, a great friend and spiritual guru. You have had my back through this entire process. Thanks for your deep understanding and unique thinking. Your insights and out-of-the-box thinking is contagious and was a force behind my ability to bring life to this book.

Last but not least, this whole endeavor would never have come about without an invitation from my coauthor, Chris McCain. Chris is a successful businessman, author, motivational speaker, and most of all a family man. Chris and I developed a relationship as his son trained with me at Beast Athletics. We discovered a common interest in reading books about personal growth, success, and unconventional thinking. He came up with the idea of writing a book about success that was focused on young athletes, and I was honored that he asked me to a part of this adventure. Chris invited me into his home and made me feel like family. In him, I have found a genuine, lifelong friend.

Without the encouragement, cooperation, and assistance of all these people, and of course the supreme creator, I would never have been able to accomplish this monumental task.

—Tuck Taylor

PREFACE

CONGRATULATIONS ON YOUR purchase of this book. By buying this book, you have made a definitive decision to begin building a life of growth and success. We, the authors of this book (Chris and Tuck), embraced this journey because we wanted to give something to young athletes to help guide them during some of the most critical years of their development.

The definite purpose of this book is to provide young athletes and their parents with a resource that will help them grow into the best version of themselves by developing a powerful mindset toward success.

As a young athlete, the earlier that you can understand and harness the power of a successful mindset, the better off you will be in tackling the many challenges that you will face in the coming years.

As adults, there is a strong tendency to develop a sense of complacency toward growth and learning as the responsibilities of parenthood set in. The focus shifts from personal growth and learning to that of our kids. We believe that by reading this book, you will not only develop the tools to raise a successful child but also find opportunities for your own personal growth. As a parent, coach, or teacher, you are a tremendous influence on your child's development. Using this book, you can become a model for your child and at the same time find new opportunities for your own success.

INTRODUCTION

IF YOU HAVE bought this book, you have likely done so with the intention of discovering tools and techniques to help you (or your child) develop a mindset of personal growth and success. This book should not be read cover to cover and then put on a shelf with other completed books. It is not a story to tell; it is not fiction. This book is a resource that should be revisited constantly and read multiple times. The contents of this book should not be viewed as part of a phase of personal growth and learning. It should be used to establish a lifelong change in the way that you think, perceive, decide, act, and live.

This is not a book that you should read for the purpose of completing it. This book should be read for thorough understanding. Let's be honest out of the gate: this book is not a long book. The length was intentional because we didn't want to scare young athletes away due to the thickness of the book. We knew athletes wouldn't want a 500 page manuscript that is difficult to follow and finish. The book is easy to read. At the same time, don't let its size fool you. The content in the book is a very powerful weapon that will change your life—but only if you read it as it was meant to be read. Read the book slowly and allow yourself to experience and connect with the words. Think about the concepts and stories and then relate them to your life. You must keep an open mind and trust in the process of owning your thoughts and controlling your own destiny. After reading the book enough times, the concepts, terms, and principles will become a natural part of your language. In developing this fluency, you should expect that it will then become easier to implement the positive mindset techniques we present and rewire your mind to think differently about the impact you have on your own life. This book is not about bringing fantasy to life; fantasies exist in a world with no limits, and we live in a world governed by both laws of nature and human-enforced laws. You can't use these tools to sit at home, think about winning the lottery, and poof! you win the lottery. There is an element of accountability that comes with learning how to be the best version of yourself through development of BEAST Thinking.

The examples in the book might relate to specific sports, but they can be applied to other sports, hobbies, as well as activities, education, relationship, parenting, and much more. The use of specific examples in the book are done so because those are the experiences we have had. The principles apply to any goals you have, whether it be sports, music, academics, or simply gaining self-awareness as a means of becoming a better person. The BEAST mindset is about personal growth for each and every individual regardless of one's definition of success.

The information in this book has been compiled from over a dozen other books that dive deep into the areas of cognition, learning, emotion, fitness, success, motivation, habits, and the human brain. The information is being presented here in a manner that will allow a younger audience (and their parents) to understand, appreciate, and engage their own natural abilities to ensure success in their lives now and in the future.

There are three foundational elements to making significant, positive, and lasting change in your life: education, engineering, and empowerment. *BEAST Thinking* was written to help you with all three pillars of successful change.

First and foremost, you must educate yourself. If you want to create change in your life, you must understand how to make change. This includes learning about the details of change and strategies for change, as well as learning stories of others' success with creating change. Knowing how the mind, brain, and body react to internal and external forces to make change is the precursor to the second pillar of change, engineering.

Once you have learned the requirements for making change, the next step is to engineer a plan for putting your new knowledge to work for you. Your plan for change will be the physical representation of your education. The engineering plan will guide you through the ups and downs of reaching your goals. You will be able to find small successes and reach major milestones as outlined by your plan. These success and milestones then become the third pillar of change, empowerment.

Empowerment, as defined by Google dictionary, is

"authority or power given to someone to do something." Once you begin to see that you can learn and engineer change into your life, you will feel a tremendous sense of empowerment. Your education and your engineering give you the authority or power over your own life to do something great. Your life builds a behavioral momentum toward the positive aspects of all that you are looking to build for yourself and those around you.

Educate.

Engineer.

Empower.

E^3.

The content in this book will directly impact the pillars of Educate and Engineer. Adding Educate and Engineer will give you the Empowerment for all your future success.

CHAPTER 1
Planting the Seeds

THE FIRST STEP to transforming into a BEAST is understanding the interwoven relationship between your thoughts, actions, habits, and circumstances.

In 1903, James Allen wrote a book titled *As a Man Thinketh*. This book was decades ahead of its time, but the content within would become the foundation of the self-help and personal develop genre. In the book, Allen wrote, "A person's mind may be likened to a garden. Whether intelligently cultivated or neglected it must and will bring forth. If no useful seeds are put into it then and abundance of useless weed seeds will fall therein and will continue to produce their kind." In Allen's text, the seeds are representative of our thoughts. What we see, hear, feel, smell, say, and think act as seeds. If we fill our minds with useful thoughts and ideas, then we can expect the garden to be fruitful. If we allow our minds to be filled with useless thoughts and ideas, then we can expect the garden to be full of weeds.

Allen's words show that we must carefully choose our

thoughts. Both our internal world and the world around us can be responsible for stimulating the mind. Caution must be taken.

By realizing and gaining deep understanding that thoughts are the roots of all your circumstances, you will soon discover your power to attract the experiences that you truly desire. You will develop a keen sense of self-awareness of your thoughts and feelings at any given moment in time. This will allow you to ensure that the subject matter of your conscious mind is that of which you are wanting. You will also come to understand why certain things have manifested in your life and why others have not. Opening your mind to the ideas in this book will leave you with a heightened sensitivity to the impact that outside stimuli have on your thoughts and ultimately your circumstances. It will be revealed to you that the outer world of circumstances is merely a reflection of the inner world of thought. This breakthrough in the way you approach life will erase previously learned limitations that you have consciously or subconsciously placed on yourself.

This shift in thinking liberates you from the faulty thought process that dominates your subconscious. Millions of people move swiftly through life with their current state as a reflection of past thought. Settling for a life based on fate and chance is a life of reactivity, not proactivity. Better life experiences grow from better thinking.

To visually represent the complete story behind mindset and its results, let's draw from the structure of a tree— let's call it the Positive Tree. A tree begins with a strong root system. Next comes the strength of the tree trunk, followed by the multidirectional branches and finally the fruit of the tree. The harmony, growth, and relationships of the tree's parts are representative of the harmony, growth, and relationships between thoughts, actions, habits, and results (or circumstances). The roots are thoughts, the trunk is actions, the branches are habits, and the fruits are the results (or circumstances of reality). Figure 1.1 details the structure of the Positive Tree.

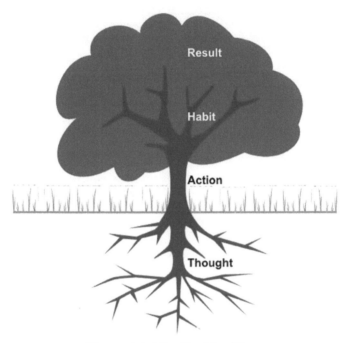

Figure 1.1. The Positive Tree.

THOUGHT

Any result, circumstance, or reality begins with a single thought, but a single thought is not enough. Henry David Thoreau once wrote, "As a single foot step will not make a path on the Earth, so a single thought will not make a pathway to the mind. To make a deep physical path we must walk again and again. To make a deep mental path we must think over and over the kind of thoughts we wish to dominate our lives." Thinking something one time is only the beginning of a new reality, just as planting a seed is the beginning of a new organism. Thoughts must be persistent, purposeful, and detailed. Much in the same way that after planting a seed, you cannot water it once and expect growth, the seeds of thought must be cultivated and cared for often.

An unhealthy person begins the road back to good health with a single thought.

An athlete begins the path to greatness with a single thought.

A student begins a journey to knowledge with a single thought.

A single thought can catalyze the beginning of a new paradigm, but it is the persistence and proactivity of continued thinking that will bring the results. Positive thought breeds positive result through positive actions and habits. Negative thought breeds negative results through negative action and habits.

Have you ever known a person who seems to dwell on the negative aspects of his or her life? A person who has lost the ability to intentionally focus on positive is providing fertile soil for seeds of thought that will bear the wrong kind of fruit, if any at all. Self-fulfilling prophecy can work in your favor, or it can work against you. It can make your wildest dreams come true, or it can bring life to your worst nightmares. Be thankful that as a conscious, mindful human being, you have complete control over the circumstances of your reality.

Positive thinking isn't just about success at work, school, or sport. It can also be the driving force behind your opportunity to attend once-in-a-lifetime sporting events or seeing your dream house become a reality. The more intentional and purposeful thought we put into something, the greater the momentum toward converting thought to reality.

This book is solely focused on the Thought (roots) level of the tree. In a future publication, we will delve into the Actions (trunk) and Habits (branch) levels.

ACTION

A tree grows from seeds and requires constant care, but it can't reach its full potential without a strong trunk to support its fruitful outcome. Success begins with positive mindset (the purpose of this book), but it requires a strong set of actions that supports the desired outcome. Thoughts and actions must be in sync with one another. A vision of success in basketball is not achieved by practicing piano, just as success in playing the piano doesn't come from shooting a basketball. The dream of becoming a master chess player is not supported by studying chemistry. Your actions must be directly related to your thoughts in order to create the right foundation for fruits to grow.

HABIT

Repeated actions become habits. Sometimes this happens by accident or subconsciously, but our focus is doing this with purpose and intent. Habits form the structure for repetition that creates the consistency or persistence required to turn thoughts into results. Some habits form easily whereas others will take significant effort (action) to become second nature.

RESULTS

> Good Thoughts + Good Actions = Good Habits = Good Results

> Bad Thoughts + Bad Actions = Bad Habits = Bad Results

For a long time, the study of human performance focused on the actions and habits that lead to enhanced performance. These actions and habits were focused mainly on the role of sport-specific training combined with strength and conditioning. The mind element is a more recent variable into the equation, but it has a significant impact on the studies of all aspects of human behavior (and performance).

Anecdotal evidence does provide us with ample evidence that mindset is the largest percentage of the three elements. Feel free to do some research of your own, but here are a few examples I can give that would be hard to argue against.

- Michael Jordan (Bulls/Wizards)
- Kobe Bryant (Lakers)
- Larry Bird (Celtics)
- Isiah Thomas (Pistons)
- Steph Curry (Warriors)
- LeBron James (Cavaliers/Heat/Lakers)
- Giannis Antetokounmpo (Bucks)
- Kyrie Irving (Cavaliers/Celtics/Nets)
- Isaiah Thomas (Celtics/Cavaliers/Lakers/Wizards)
- Russel Westbrook (Thunder/Rockets)
- James Harden (Thunder/Rockets)

@beast_thinking_

- Tom Brady (Patriots)
- Peyton Manning (Colts/Broncos)
- Venus and Serena Williams (tennis)

This is a very impressive list of names, but it's also a widely varying list of people when it comes to physical traits, athletic skills, speed, size, and strength. With so many variances between these athletes, is it possible to come up with a common trait that they all share? In fact, it is possible. The common thread among them is mindset. Again, it would take a lot of scientific study and hundreds of hours of interviews to dig into the psyche of each of these elite level athletes, but without any study, you can watch them play. Across sports, genders, races, and widely varying physical traits, it is impossible to identify a common physical characteristic among the greatest. That tells us the commonality among them is not something we can see on the playing field. Some quick research into any of these athletes would reveal that each possesses an uncommonly strong thirst for success that is made up by his or her willingness to learn, put forth effort, be wrong, and most important fail.

The best of any field, whether it be sports, academics, medicine, business, or parenting, is willing and eager to fail. Failure presents an opportunity to learn, and learning is the foundation for continued growth. Sports and academics are the easiest to see. Who is willing to take that final shot? Who wants that final shot? Who is eager for rigor and difficulty in the classroom?

Where does the willingness to learn, grow, be wrong, and fail fit into the mix with the traditional characteristics of skill and physical development? This is a tough question to answer scientifically because of the magnitude of the study required to provide a definitive answer, but what is more important than a scientific study is your personal opinion. Figure 1.2 shows a pie chart with the three elements that impact human performance: skill, physical development, and mindset.

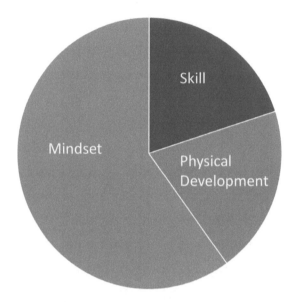

Figure 1.2. The three elements of human performance include mindset, skill development, and physical development.

The chart shows that mindset is the largest impact on human performance (60 percent), whereas skill and physical development are equal to one another (20 percent each). This chart was not created from a scientific process or as a result of some mathematical computation. It was created as a means of helping you form your belief system around skill, physical development, and mindset. Do you agree with this chart? How would you study or test the three characteristics to determine which had the greatest impact? The percentage values assigned to the three elements are not as important as understanding the three elements and their interactions. Calculating specific values for the elements and their impact on human performance would require significant, long-term study of athletes, and therefore at this point, they are simply subjective values.

Let's try this a different a way. Figure 1.3 shows skill, physical development, and mindset being dropped into a machine that will then create a model for human performance. What does that outcome look like? Which of the resulting models do you believe?

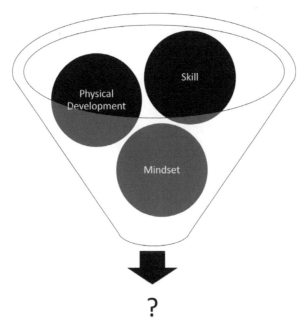

Figure 1.3. If you combine skill, physical development, and mindset, what kind of model best represents their interaction for impacting human performance?

Would you consider any one of the three to be more important than the other two? Are they all equal? Do you have to possess one before either of the others? Does one element impact another? Can one of the elements be missing and still allow for success?

In the following few pages, we are going to provide some sample models. Look at each model and think about its underlying meaning about the interaction between the elements of mindset, physical development, and skill. The samples we provide are meant to help you get a better understanding of your own opinion and attitude toward the three elements. Each of the models has characteristics that are valid and valuable, but each also has characteristics that are arguable. There isn't a correct model; it's an exercise in self-discovery.

Let's look at the first sample model. Figure 1.4 shows a model that reflects mindset as the foundation for human performance. On top of mindset is physical development, and then the top of the pyramid is skill. This model places more emphasis on mindset than on skill. Do you believe that mindset is a bigger factor toward success than skill? Do you believe that mindset and physical development together are enough for success?

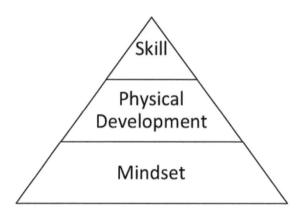

Figure 1.4. Human performance model with a foundation in mindset, leading to physical development and culminating with skill.

@beast_thinking_

Would you change anything about this model?

Figure 1.5 reflects a human performance model in which all three characteristics are equal to one another and are part of a cyclical process. There is no specific starting point in the process, and each of the elements impacts and is impacted by another of the elements. Do you agree with this model?

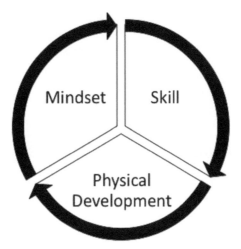

Figure 1.5. The cycle of human development with equal elements of mindset, skill, and physical development.

Would you change anything on this model? Do you agree with the direction of the arrows? Would you make them bidirectional? Would you change the location of the elements in the cycle?

The final model is shown in figure 2.5. Figure 2.5 reflects the three elements of human performance as individual, equal entities with overlap between two and three of the elements.

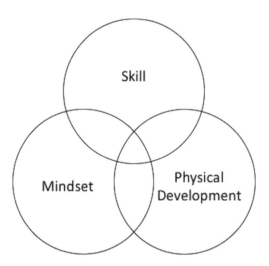

Figure 2.5. Mindset, physical development, and skill as equal and overlapping elements for human performance.

What would you change about this model? Would you change the size of each circle to reflect a difference in importance? Would you change the amount that the circles overlap to reflect the combined power the overlap as it relates to chances of success?

You will find the BEAST Thinking social media handle on the bottom of each page. Throughout the book, we will invite you to ask, answer, and share your questions, answers, thoughts, and ideas with the BEAST Thinking community using Twitter, Instagram, and Facebook.

Use this page to create your own model. Share it with your parents, teammates, and even the authors and other readers.

The impact of mindset, mentality, thought, meditation, and more is not limited to sports. Although this book focuses mainly on the impact to the teenage athlete (and parents), the concepts you learn here are applicable to education, business, and even personal relationships.

The times are changing as elite athletes share personal stories of success with details on the importance of mindset and mental preparation. These stories make young athletes sit up and take notice. In addition, science is leading to new breakthroughs in the areas of neuroscience that are providing deeper insights into human performance.

CHAPTER 2
Brain versus Mind

A S YOU READ this book, there are highly complex functions taking place between your eyes and through your brain. Letters are recognized as words, defined, processed, and understood within context in less than a second. These incredibly fast-occurring events are the work of your physical brain.

Before we go any further, I want to provide you with the sense of relief in knowing that this chapter is not going to be completely focused on the anatomy and function of the human brain. Surely you will get enough biology and anatomy study in school. However, it is important to go through some basics in order to set the stage for the "brain versus mind" discussion in this chapter and the remainder of the material in this book, which is focused on how our minds are the source of power behind all our success. Knowing the information that follows will help define the difference between brain and mind.

Think of a car that you know goes extremely fast: Ferrari,

Lamborghini, Porsche, Bugatti, or (if you are a *Need for Speed* fan) the highly sought-after Koenigsegg. These cars represent incredible pieces of machinery that are capable of performing incredible things in a race (or car chase). No matter which car you might choose from this list, the one thing that will be required to get maximum performance is a driver who can demand that performance. The driver must be able to control the car. He must be able to use each of its optimized pieces to get the most he can from the car. The driver must understand the sounds of the engine at different speeds and gears, read the gauges, smell the tires, and feel the vibrations of the car. The driver makes all the difference in the success of the car.

Let's assume, however, that the driver of this car is not an experienced race car driver or professional driver of some sort. Instead, let's put a sixteen-year-old driver in the driver's seat, and let's assume that this driver just got his license this morning. There are three potential outcomes from this scenario.

Scenario number one, the least likely of all the scenarios, is that somehow this newly licensed driver gets in the car and performs exactly like the professional driver or close to it. Given the newness of the driving experience and the lack of familiarity with the car, this is an extremely unlikely scenario and certainly not one that I would expect.

Scenario number two places the sixteen-year-old driver behind the wheel of this car, and without hesitation, he begins to push the car to its limits. There is no plan, no learning, just pedal to the metal. Certainly this can't end in a good way. This driver is most likely to end up crashing the car, damaging both the car and himself.

The last scenario, number three, is the most likely. The sixteen-year-old driver will get into the car and drive, but he will reach limits at which he becomes uncomfortable for fear of crashing (failing). This keeps the driver safe and protected, but he will never experience the full potential of the car, and therefore all of its superior craftsmanship will be wasted.

Your brain is an elite, expensive, and highly specialized car. Your mind is a driver.

The race car analogy is not meant to describe fearlessness versus caution. The analogy is meant to show how the physical brain (car) in all of us is an incredible tool to be used. But in order to get maximum potential, we have to use our logical minds to put the right information and thoughts (driver) into it.

The brain, like the race car, has highly specialized components that allow it to perform with incredible speed, efficiency, and power. There are different regions in the brain that are responsible for different activities, and there's a large network of neurons (neural network) to process the various events that go on in your life (external stimuli). Using the word *large* is actually an understatement when it comes to describing the neural network of the brain, considering the fact that there are over one hundred billion nerve cells, called neurons, and up to one quadrillion connections, called synapses.

Neurons are highly specialized cells that are responsible for transmitting signals throughout the body. Figure 2.1 shows the structure of a neuron.

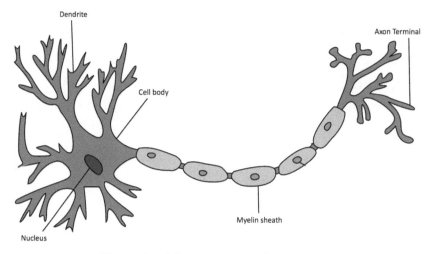

Figure 2.1. The structure of a neuron.

Aside from the nucleus and soma (cell body), the neuron has two highly distinguishable extensions, called dendrites and axons. The dendrites are extensions of a neuron that receive electrical signals and conduct them toward the cell body. The axons are extensions of a neuron that conduct electrical signals away from the cell body and toward the cell body of another neuron. Neurons transmit electrical signals through the brain and body to complete motor functions, either on purpose or as a reaction. When you walk, neurons are transmitting signals through a path of neurons or neural path that tells your body to perform the movements necessary to walk. Even though you don't have to think about the specific motor skills required to walk, you are still voluntarily performing the behavior. The neurons transmit signals extremely fast. Can you remember a time when you accidently exposed your body to a painful stimulus? Maybe you stepped on a Lego or touched something very hot. In either case, you didn't have to tell yourself to lift your foot

@beast_thinking_

or pull your hand away, and it didn't take you a long time to eliminate the cause of the immediate pain. Whether walking or reacting to pain, neurons are firing through brain and body.

For the purposes of gaining a deeper understanding of how we humans develop habits, and more specifically how you as an athlete develop elite skills, you must understand the function of the myelin sheath. In figure 2.1, you can see the myelin sheath surrounding the axon as if it were a protective barrier. It is actually better than a protective barrier—it is a membrane that helps speed the electrical transmissions that occur in the brain. The insulating nature of myelin is useful for simple motor function (e.g., walking), sensory function (e.g., feeling pain), and cognition (e.g., learning/recalling). When your body performs a specific movement over and over again, myelin builds to help speed up the electrical impulses required to perform the movement. In sports, this is often referred to as muscle memory, but it is much more than simply development of sports because it plays an important role in development of language and even our daily habits.

Later in the book, we will discuss the idea of deep practice for the intent of building myelin for those behaviors that are critical to your success as an athlete.

The billions of neurons in your brain's neural network are spread across the different areas of the brain. The areas of the brain are responsible for different aspects of your everyday life. Figure 2.1 shows the different areas of the brain.

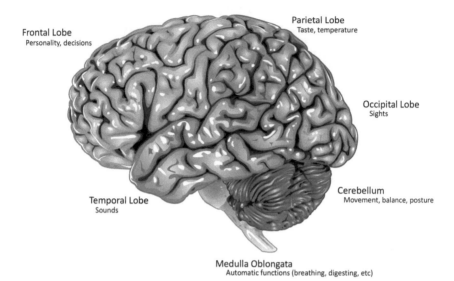

Figure 2.2. The areas of the physical brain.

The parietal lobe is part of the brain's cortex and is responsible for a variety of functions, including processing sensory information like taste and temperature.

The occipital lobe is used to help process and correctly understand what your eyes are seeing. The occipital lobe processes visual information extremely fast. As you walk down the street and casually see people, cars, and buildings, the occipital lobe processes this visual information. On the basketball court or football field, as opponents run, jump, and defend at various speeds, the occipital lobe processes this information.

The temporal lobe is used to help process and correctly understand what your ears are hearing. It receives information like sounds and speech from your ears and interprets the sounds for what they are: meaningful speech or noise. The temporal lobe makes sense of sound. As you walk down the street, you hear people talking, cars honking, motorcycles driving by, or construction on a building. On the basketball court or football field, you hear offensive plays, defense formations, a ball bouncing, or a horn blowing. All of this information is processed and given meaning by the temporal lobe.

The frontal lobe is responsible for your personality, and you use it every day to make decisions. These decisions can be simple things like what to have for breakfast or what to wear, or they can be more important things like studying for a test or training for sports. The frontal lobe is where we perform our higher mental processes like speaking fluently, planning, and setting goals. This is a critical area of the brain for BEAST Thinking. It is here where you can focus great attention in an effort to help you achieve maximum results as a young, developing athlete.

The cerebellum sits at the back of the brain behind the brain stem (where the spinal cord meets the brain). It gets information from the sensory systems, the spinal cord, and other areas of the brain that control motor functions (movement). The cerebellum coordinates voluntary movements such as posture, balance, and coordination, resulting in smooth and fluid activity. It is also vital in the learning of new movements. The cerebellum is a small portion of the brain (about 10 percent of total weight), but it is made up of almost 50 percent of the brain's neurons. That should tell you how important the cerebellum is.

The medulla oblongata is a cone-shaped mass of nerves that controls involuntary (autonomic) functions. The involuntary functions include actions such digestion, heartbeat, sneezing, and breathing. You don't have to try to digest food. You don't have to make yourself sneeze. You don't have to constantly remind yourself to breathe. These things happen automatically. However, in the last chapter of the book, we will teach you how to breathe with purpose as a means of learning how to focus as part of mindful meditation.

If the brain is the mass that sits within the skull, then what is the mind? What is the difference between the two? Can we use the words *brain* and *mind* interchangeably? The remainder of this chapter will answer these questions.

The previous few pages introduced you to the layout and function of the physical brain. As I promised, it was short and sweet. But now the focus will shift away from the physical brain and toward the logical mind.

The mind is the equivalent of the driver that is put into the supercar. With the right driver, the supercar is a thing of beauty. With the right driver, all the superior engineering of the engine, tires, body, and interior come together to create an elite level of success. With the wrong driver, all that is unrealized or even destroyed. Just like you can put the right driver in the car, you can put the right information into your brain.

If you owned that supercar and were going to let someone drive it, think about the type of driver you would want.

- Would you want someone with a positive attitude or a negative attitude?
- Would you want a driver who thinks carelessly or one who plans properly for success?

- Would you want a driver who is ignorant to the specifications of the car or a driver who has studied all of its details?

Your mind, unlike the driver, is not something you can touch or see. Your mind represents the conscious thoughts, beliefs, and perceptions that you have in your life. Figure 2.2 shows the logical mind and the physical brain.

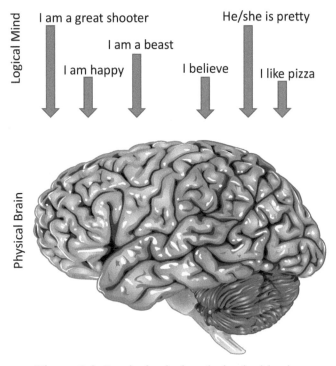

Figure 2.3. Logical mind and physical brain.

As a child in school, you are exposed to new information. You accept much of this information as fact. For example, at some point in your life, all of the information below was new to you:

- $10 + 10 = 20$
- $10 \times 10 = 100$
- The Earth is round.
- People cannot fly, but airplanes can.

When this information came to you through a teacher, a book, a worksheet, or some other method, your brain processed the information. At this point in your life, you can pull back some of that information as fact, and probably within less than a second. These are facts that were created for you, given to you, and are ingrained in your brain.

So where does the mind fit into this picture?

Let's say that you are in the first grade, and you are having your first ever math test. The test doesn't go too well, and you score a 70 percent. Your mind may register this result in one of two ways: "I am not good at math," or "I need to study more." You are in first grade, so it is unlikely that your first inclination is going to be a sprint to the math worksheets to get some more practice. It is much easier to resort to the idea that you are not good at math. These thoughts are not driven by the brain; they are the driver of the brain. By constantly using the mind to make yourself a victim to math, you are creating a fact that is stored in your brain just as $10 + 10 = 20$ would be stored. You are choosing to put a subpar driver at the wheel of an incredible supercar when you put negative ideas into the brain.

Negativity placed into our minds does not have to happen over a long period of time to be bad for our chances of success. Even short spurts of a negative mindset can have huge impact.

One day in the summer of 2016, I was doing a shooting workout with one of the kids on the basketball team I coach. The kid, who was twelve years old at the time, also happened to be my son, Hayden. Hayden had not shot in a few days, so he was excited to be on the court and "get in some makes," as we like to call it. We don't like to shoot the ball; we like to make the ball. (Note the mind trick in the words we use). The shooting session started out as normal with one hundred makes of form shooting from right in front of the hoop, followed by one hundred makes of form shooting from each side of the hoop. The final phase of the warm-up is one hundred makes from in front of the hoop approximately six feet away. He completes four hundred makes before he steps back.

After the first four hundred makes, Hayden moved back to make shots from ten to twelve feet. He started with a side-to-side slide, hands-ready, baseline-to-wing drill. As was his normal shooting, he made ten out roughly fifteen shots. Next up was elbow makes—same side-to-side, hands-ready routine, with a similar result of ten out of fourteen.

Things were progressing fine until he hit the opposite baseline-to-wing session. The session started off with consecutive misses. I could see in his face that frustration was mounting even after two misses. Then a third miss. A fourth miss. A fifth miss. Hayden is an extremely driven twelve-year-old. He loves basketball despite only having been playing for two years, but he loves everything about the game. He loves the process, he loves the games, he loves to train, he loves to watch the game, and he loves to make videos about the game. But as powerful as that love can be, it doesn't take much to sour a training session because the mind is a superpower.

Finally a made shot, but then a sixth miss.

"My shot is trash," he uttered.

A seventh miss.

An eighth miss.

"Ugh. Trash," he repeated.

After a ninth miss, he was on the verge of a massive meltdown.

At this point, I couldn't watch any more. Sure, there are some things I can correct with his form. Use more legs, follow through forward, put more spin on the ball—these would have been useful suggestions. But it would not have mattered because his mind had already driven the brain to proceed with failure because his shot "was trash." The mind drives the brain, and the brain drives the body. The brain will do as the mind wills, and the body will follow.

I grabbed the ricocheted ninth miss and walked over to Hayden with the ball under my arm. The scowl on his face was worth a thousand more misses. I talked to him for a few minutes about his warm-up, his drive, and his uniqueness as a twelve-year-old who was so motivated to succeed in this game that he loved. I could still see that his face was not quite yet convinced that he could make shots.

"Close your eyes," I told him. "You are a great shooter, Hayden. You have worked for two years to ensure that you have good form. You don't push the ball or launch the ball like many kids who play this game. You have stayed the course, and you have been through the struggles of not having the strength to shoot from as far away as others. And through all of this, you have so much more to do to reach your goals. You are a great shooter, Hayden."

His face softened a bit more.

From here, I had him repeat "I am a great shooter" several times. He opened his eyes. The look on his face was no longer one of extreme frustration; it was one of determination. I told him to keep saying it as he shot this last and final round of the session.

"I am a great shooter." First miss.
"I am a great shooter." First make.
"I am a great shooter." Second make.
"I am a great shooter." Third make.
"I am a great shooter." Fourth make.
"I am a great shooter." Fifth make.
"I am a great shooter." Second miss.
"I am a great shooter." Sixth make.
"I am a great shooter." Seventh make.
"I am a great shooter." Eighth make.
"I am a great shooter." Ninth make.
"I am a great shooter." Tenth make. Ten of twelve.

After missing a number of shots, Hayden's perception of his abilities became negative. However, perception is open to change through the power of the logical mind. In the book *Super Brain* by Deepak Chopra and Rudolph Tanzi, the authors state, "Perception isn't passive. You are not simply receiving a fixed, given reality. You are shaping it. Self-awareness changes perception. The more aware you are, the more power you have over your reality." Through a positive (or negative) mind, you must be accountable for your own experiences and outcomes.

This is the power of the mind. This is where the mind allows us to drive the brain. In this example, with my help, Hayden became self-aware of the positive aspects of his shooting ability. That awareness and subsequent positive mindset, combined with the auditory affirmation of "I am a great shooter," reshaped his perception, and in the end it altered his reality.

You might read this and think this is an isolated incident, or maybe the earlier missed shots prepped him to shoot better. This type of thinking is what we would call a fixed mindset, and we'll talk about this in the next chapter. I can assure you we have had other shooting sessions where this same philosophy has worked. We are very big on tracking data. We want to know that mindset is producing actions that get results. On another occasion, we were doing stationary shooting from the free throw line using a rebounding machine that I created. It works like a life-sized pop-a-shot game: you shoot, and the balls roll right back into the shooting pocket.

One evening, Hayden and I were taking turns shooting. The goal was one hundred makes, shooting twenty shots at a time. Here is how the session went.

> First attempt: 13 out of 20
> Second attempt: 12 out of 20 (total: 25 of 40, 62 percent)
> Third attempt: 11 out of 20 (total: 36 of 60, 60 percent)
> Fourth Attempt: 9 out of 20 (total: 45 of 80, 56 percent)

Frustration set in. Reset the mind. Remember the mantra: "I am a great shooter." The mind will drive the brain. The brain will drive the body.

> Fifth attempt: 17 out of 20 (total: 62 of 100, 62 percent)
> Sixth attempt: 19 out of 20 (total: 81 of 120, 67 percent)

At this point, we got called in for dinner, but there was no doubt that his change in mindset was going to make for continued success. The mind will drive the brain. The brain will drive the body.

Understanding and using these mind techniques are especially critical for athletes in situations where precious moments of concentration are required for success, such as shooting free throws in a basketball game or standing at bat in baseball or softball.

Stepping up to shoot free throws in a basketball game is a perfect time for the mind to wander to the path of "What if I miss?" or "I could miss." In these situations, no matter the amount of practice you have had, if your mind is setting you up to fail, then your chances of success will certainly diminish. Similarly, in baseball and softball, if your mind is more focused on the opportunity to strike out, then your chances of success will diminish. As an athlete, in these situations you must use the power of your mind to convince your body that success is the only outcome. If the mind is so focused on the success outcome that failure can't occupy your mind, then the body will be more willing to follow through on success instead of failure.

I tell all of my players to keep their free throw routine short. Step up to the free throw line, take a dribble, and shoot. The longer you place an athlete in a pressure situation, the longer the mind has to try to stay focused on the desired outcome—or worse, the longer the mind has to focus on a negative outcome. In baseball and softball, it is much more difficult because the amount of time spent in the batter's box is also dependent on how long the pitcher holds the ball.

A basketball player is fouled with six seconds left in the game, and his team is down by one point. He has practiced these shots thousands of times. If his mind is filled with thoughts of negative, then despite the practice, his body is not likely to follow through with successful muscle memory. Negative thoughts would include the following.

- What if I miss these free throws?
- I suck at free throws.
- We are going to lose this game.
- I missed my last three free throws.
- I really shouldn't be the one shooting these. _____ is much better than I am at free throws.

These types of thoughts are certainly not the right mindset. A simple mantra during these situations can help push these thoughts out of the mind. Positive mindset thinking would include the following.

- I am a great free throw shooter.
- We will win this game.

The outcome of success is much more likely with these types of thoughts. Let the mind control the brain, and the brain will control the body.

In baseball and softball, the mindset is very important because you are guaranteed to be in a position of mind-driven success and failure. A softball player is playing in a major national tournament or showcase. At these events, college scouts are watching, and all the players are the best in their regions. In softball, you know several batters (minutes) before you have to step up to the plate and perform. This gives the mind more critical minutes to develop the potential outcomes. However, remember that you are in control of your mind. As the batter waits for her turn at bat, her mind can skid into a negative mindset with thoughts like this.

- I suck at hitting. (Kids love to use "I suck at ___.")
- I haven't been hitting the ball well.
- I struck out last time.
- In my last at bat, I hit a short one right to first base
- What if someone important is watching, and I strike out?

With all the time waiting until her at bat, if her mind is running through the thoughts above, then stepping up to the plate is going to amplify these thoughts. The body will then follow with reduced effort or poor mechanics.

But what if the time waiting to bat was spent in positive thinking? Positive thinking includes thoughts like the following.

- I am a great hitter.
- My mechanics are exactly what they need to be for me to make the right contact with the ball.
- I am a fast runner. I will make contact, and I can make it to first.

In both of these situations, the basketball player and the softball player, the mind is a critical factor in the outcome. Players must use their minds to construct success without the fear of failure. Not being afraid to fail allows the brain to diminish the impact of its biggest enemy. We will talk more about failure in chapter 3.

Rumor has it that Michael Jordan used to play out games in his head before the games even happened. Do you think he ever lost one of those games in his head? Do you think he ever missed a last-second shot in his mind? Perhaps this was part of his secret to having one of the most success-driven minds in the history of the game of basketball. Many experts agree that although Michael was physically an elite athlete, his mind was what earned him the title of the greatest of all time (GOAT).

As powerful as the mind-brain-body trio can be, there are certainly limits to which this principle can apply. You can't use positive mindset to drive the brain to get the body to break the laws of physics. For example, Hayden is only five feet tall. No matter how many times he tells himself that he can dunk on a ten-foot-tall basketball goal, there is no way the laws of physics will allow that with his current muscular structure. In the same vein, you couldn't sit around all day and say, "I can fly," and then flap your arms to fly away.

@beast_thinking_

There are limitations within the realm of the possible to the positive mindset.

A tricky part to this is understanding the real limitations versus the self-imposed limitations, or limitations that are driven by fear and not physical impossibility.

Imagine you are jumping up onto a platform. After each attempt, the platform is raised by one inch. In this experiment, there are two events that will occur at some point: you think you won't make the jump (fear-based limitation), and you won't make the jump (law of physics-based limitation). Which event happens first varies from person to person. The differentiating factor is mindset. Where would you stop attempting to jump on to the platform? We will discuss fear later in the book.

In Hayden's specific case, this was certainly not his first time shooting a basketball. Hayden spends hundreds of hours working on his shot, including going to bed early several days a week so he can wake up and get five hundred makes in before school. In this case, the physical capability of making the basketball is within the realm of possibility. The muscles in his body that are coordinated by the brain have been trained to make the proper movement to experience the success of a made shot. This allows the mind to be a powerful force behind the outcome of the event. Certainly, you can miss as many shots as you want to if your mindset is to miss on purpose. So why is it crazy to think that you can't make as many as you want if your mindset is to make on purpose?

Your mind will respond to something that doesn't exist, even believing it to be true. Remember how $10 + 10 = 20$ at one point didn't exist in your mind, and then there was a point where it did exist, and it was true? You don't want 10 + 10 to equal 20—you know it. You can see it in your mind. In this same manner, you should see your success in your mind.

In her book *You Are a Badass,* author Jen Sincero writes, "You need to go from wanting to change your life to deciding to change your life." Making a decision to do something is the conscious mind formulating actions to be carried through the brain and to the body. It doesn't take external events, good or bad, to bring change to your life. It doesn't take luck, good or bad, to bring change to your life. All it takes is self-awareness and a strong, positive mind to make a conscious decision for change. This sounds easy, and it might make you wonder why more people don't do it. It is easy in today's world to get distracted, and most people are so in tune with the distractions of life that their minds can't envision the success that is available to them. Jen goes on to say, "You created the reality you now exist in with your thoughts, which means you can use the very same power of thought to change it."

The more you establish the success in your mind, the easier it is for the brain to drive the body to perform the actions that will make success a reality.

In 1938, a young author by the name of Napoleon Hill wrote a book titled *Outwitting the Devil.* The book remained unpublished for seventy-two years. *Outwitting the Devil* was not Napoleon Hill's first book. His first book, *Think and Grow Rich,* was a successful publication that was published during one of the most critical times in US history, the Great Depression. So why did this book remain hidden? According to those close to the Hill family, it was supposedly hidden and locked away by Hill's wife because she was fearful of the book's impact and the reaction it would cause.

In *Outwitting the Devil*, Napoleon Hill has a conversation with the devil. Before we get into a few of the important parts, let me first assure you that Hill did not actually have a conversation with the devil. The premise of the book, as his wife suggested, is to draw up strong feelings and promote deep thinking. The devil is a term Hill uses synonymously with anything negative—negative thinking, fear, failure, laziness, complacency, anger, distrust, and more. The book even begins with the following quote.

> FEAR is the tool of a man-made devil. Self-confident faith in one's self is both the man-made weapon which defeats this devil and the man-made tool which builds triumphant life. And it is more than that. It is a link to the irresistible forces of the universe which stand behind a man who does not believe in failure and defeat as being anything but temporary experiences.

From this quote, we know that Hill is constructing the devil to be a powerful representation of the negative. Later in his interview, Hill questions the devil about his physical appearance and where he lives. The devil says,

> I consist of negative energy, and I live in the minds of people who fear me … I control a part of the brain space of every human being. The

amount of space I occupy in each individual's mind depends upon how little and what sort of thinking that person does. As I have told you, I cannot entirely control any person who thinks.

I hope that as you read this, you notice how Hill uses the term *brain* and *mind* interchangeably. I also hope you notice the inaccuracy in doing so. We showed you earlier in this chapter that brain and mind are two different pieces to the human being and are not synonymous with each other. Nevertheless, the point that Hill is making is still very powerful. If we do not use our minds in the right way, or if we do not use them at all, then we are accepting the negativity and living in the fear of which Hill's devil speaks.

If we use our minds not just to think but to think positively, then we can prevent Hill's devil from occupying any space in our minds.

Remember that in this situation, the devil is not representing a demon character that is guarding the gates of hell. The devil is representative of the negative things that can dwell in our minds—or worse, be put there by others, or even created on our own.

Outwitting the Devil may have been written more than seven decades ago, but the full extent of its content is very relevant in today's world, especially considering the advances in science and research that have proven the underlying power of a positive mind. You are in control of your mind. You are in control of the thoughts that you entertain in your mind. You are in control of the impact other people have on you.

Your mind is your greatest weapon in helping shape the future and achieve everything your mind can create.

Will you be one of the people who doesn't think for themselves or uses one's mind to breed negative thinking? Or will you take control of your mind and use it to lay the roots of positive thinking?

Becoming a powerful force in your own life is not an easy task. Napoleon Hill's devil stated that he lives in ninety-eight out of every one hundred people. Even though this number has little if any scientific relevance, it is probably not too far off from the reality of how many people are able to build their lives around positive thinking and purposeful intent. Our hope, as authors of this book, is that we can give you the knowledge and understanding of how to take ownership of your mindset and your subsequent success, as well as give you the tools and motivation to make this happen.

The fact that you are even reading this book separates you from others whose negative minds won't open them to the possibilities that are addressed in this book. But reading the book alone is not enough. You have to accept these ideas and use the tools we give you to bring them into your life, or more accurately, into your mind.

You might be familiar with the mathematical concept called the transitive property of equality.

If $A = B$ and $B = C$, then $A = C$

In similar fashion, there is a transitive property to transformation.

> **If the mind controls the brain and the brain controls the body, then the mind controls the body.**

Your mind is your most powerful tool for creating change, discovering opportunity, and producing the results you want in your life.

CHAPTER 3
Mindset

WHAT IS A MINDSET?

A S WE COVERED in chapter 2, your mind is the logical construct that drives the operation of the brain and body. So what is a Mindset? A mindset—or rather, *your* mindset—is the overall state or pattern of thought, beliefs, ideas, and perceptions that are in your mind. Your mindset drives the way you live your life. Your mindset establishes the tone for the way you perceive, respond, interact, approach, fail, succeed, and more. Your mindset can be seen in your personality as well as in your definitions of success and failure. Mindset is the central part to all areas of life, including self-awareness, education, relationships, religion, career, and athletics.

> Note: Pause here and read this a few times so that you are very clear.

Your mindset is determined by you.

Up until this point in your life you have been shaped by your environment to think a certain way, see the world a certain way, and respond in certain ways. But as an eager and mindful teenager, the information you are about to read will now give you the education you need to change the way you see yourself and the world around you. What you do with the information you are about to read is entirely up to you. Your response to this is not determined by your parents, your genetics, or your history. Your mindset is a willful, purposeful, and determined choice you make.

> Your mindset is determined by you.
> One more time for good measure.
> Your mindset is determined by you.

THE TWO MINDSETS

In her book *Mindset: The New Psychology of Success,* author Carol S. Dweck defines two types of mindsets: fixed and growth. One mindset may be dominant, but it is possible for people to identify with both mindsets under differing conditions. With this book, our goal is that by being educated on the power of mindset, you will be able to make the decision to be a growth mindset individual in all areas of your work.

FIXED MINDSET

The fixed mindset believes that all aspects of our personality, intelligence, and abilities are given to us and cannot be changed. Fixed mindset people are less likely to believe in the value of hard work, persistence, and failure. It is in the fixed mindset where we most commonly see people falling into the misconception of "the natural." Have you ever heard an adult, or even other kids, say something like this?

- "That kid is a natural athlete."
- "Her game is so natural."
- "She is so smart without even studying."

You may have heard people say this about others, or even about you. Clearly you cannot discount that athletic or scholastic performance is easier for some kids than it is for others, but this type of mindset can be extremely damaging and harmful, as we will see in the coming pages.

The Rise (and Fall) of the Gifted Child. That's what I would call a book I could write entirely on this subject.

It's unfortunate that many of today's schools and school systems focus on labeling children. I can't help but cringe every time I hear people talk about their child being "gifted" or taking "gifted" class. In her book Grit, Angela Duckworth states that "mythologizing natural talent lets us all off the hook. It lets us relax into the

> **Labels are the fixed mindset way of establishing limitations.**

status quo." By this, Duckworth means that accepting the

natural talent idea makes it easy for us to make excuses to not work hard. Labels are the fixed mindset way of establishing limitations. If we can attribute someone else's success to something we don't have, then we can justify why we don't have similar success. That robs us of potential experiences, and this is an awful way to move through life.

It is difficult for fixed mindset individuals to look at the success of others and put together an image of hard work, effort, sacrifice, challenges, obstacles, and repeated failure. It is much easier to chalk it up to innate gifts and go about their way.

After a talk I gave in Charlotte, North Carolina, one of the audience members approached me with a heavy dose of thanks and praise. He explained that my talk helped him realize that his son, having been labeled as gifted throughout his schooling, was not outgoing and never wanted to engage in anything new other than schoolwork. Although they were certainly proud of his achievements in school, they were puzzled by his "inability" to do other things.

I use the term *inability* because that is what the father said to me. But it wasn't an inability to do other things; it was an unwillingness to do anything that would jeopardize the long-held label that he was gifted.

There is a common misconception that all children labeled as gifted, or all smart children, are growth mindset children. This could not be further from the truth. Even beyond my newfound friend in Charlotte, I have seen it in kids whom I have taught and coached. The truth is that by applying that label of "gifted" to our kids, we are establishing their identities with a single word that is backed by a single set of actions (reading, studying, researching, shooting, hitting, throwing, etc.). By continuing to label them through many years of school, we cement the idea. Furthermore, we cement a set of character traits that will forever define them and the effort they are willing to put forth. Angela Duckworth writes, "Without effort, your talent is nothing more than your unmet potential. Without effort, your skill is nothing more than what you could have done but didn't."

Challenges

Fixed mindset people are quick to avoid challenges. By believing that traits are fixed and can't be changed, these people see no reason to take on challenges. Especially in the case of the naturals, they will avoid anything that could jeopardize their status as being naturally gifted. In their minds, or as they've been told, if they have a natural ability, then nothing should be difficult when it comes to that ability. To maintain that sense of giftedness fixed mindset, people will stay away from challenges that might result in no longer being seen as special and natural talents.

Can you think of a time when you or someone you knew avoided trying something new? Maybe it was a new sport or an advanced class. In athletics, this can happen often because athletes can be challenged to do or try other things. With a fixed mindset, people who are good in one subject or sport will not participate in something different. They lack the desire, will, and mindset to embrace a challenge because of the overarching fear of failing. The failure then leads to a discovery that their natural abilities are limited.

Obstacles

Running into obstacles is a big problem for fixed mindset people. Obstacles, like challenges, are opportunities for abilities to be called into question. Fixed mindset people get very defensive and give up easily and quickly when there are obstacles that need to be overcome. Obstacles that prevent success to a fixed mindset are often met with a multitude of excuses aimed at outside forces. To people with a fixed mindset, obstacles are someone else's fault, not their own. Think of a high school athlete with a fixed mindset who doesn't make the varsity team or doesn't get enough playing time. How does the athlete respond to these obstacles? Typically, it's by blaming the coach. And let's be honest: in many cases, it isn't just the athlete but a fixed mindset parent as well.

"That coach doesn't know what he's doing."

"I don't understand why coach doesn't play me."

"We need to find a coach that sees and appreciates my child's ability."

These are just a few examples of the fixed mindset excuses that players (or parents) make in the face of sports-related obstacles.

This is extremely common in today's amateur travel sports like basketball and softball. As money pours in for the organizations that oversee amateur sports, the culture continues to foster misconceptions and fixed mindsets as players bounce from team to team, looking for where they can get the most playing time or, more important, the most exposure. Rather than coaches being realistic with parents and players, they create false senses of security by attaching labels to players in the hopes that players can live up to the label. The coaches seek to create winning programs that in the long run benefit the coaches and the organizing body more than the players.

Effort

In many cases, challenges and obstacles are perceived to be harder than they really are, and with a little effort, they can be mastered. But effort is not something in which fixed mindset people believe. Effort is often seen as pointless.

Let's dive into an example. Imagine there is a player on your basketball team (or pick a different sport and insert the necessary actions). We can call him Ashley. Ashley is one of your best players and perhaps one of the people whom many would consider to be "naturally" good. Ashley is tall, fast, and athletic. Ashley can jump high enough to dunk, shoot from deep, rebound, and pass to anyone from anywhere. When the ball goes in to play until the final horn, the whole game seems so easy to Ashley. But Ashley's play is highly individualistic. Ashley doesn't rely on teammates and isn't supportive of the team when things are going wrong.

During practice one day, the coach has decided to run a new drill. This drill requires coordinated effort from all five players in the drill. It is a complicated drill that requires maximum effort and concentration. In the first few attempts on the drill, Ashley is causing the team to fail. It's a new concept for Ashley, who is used to relying only on individual effort to be successful. Everyone on the team and all the coaches are watching. Ashley continues to be in the wrong spot at the wrong time while his teammates continue to do the drill properly. The coach steps in to say something to Ashley about effort and performance. After a few more attempts, and subsequent failures, Ashley becomes defensive about the drill and then says one or more of the following.

- "This drill is stupid."
- "We don't do this in a game."
- "Why aren't we just shooting the ball?"
- "I'll dunk on all of you."

Ashley's fixed mindset won't allow the idea that failure is something to learn from and that there is value in learning to work as a team to be successful. Can you venture a guess as to why Ashley wasn't willing to try the drill anymore? Why did Ashley quit so quickly? The short answer is that Ashley likely has a fixed mindset. The medium answer is that Ashley has a fixed mindset, doesn't take on challenges easily, and quits quickly in the face of obstacles. But there is even more to it than that. Looking deeper into this scenario, there are a lot of things going on that are mounting up against Ashley's fixed mindset. We already mentioned the challenge and the obstacles, but the other factors at play here are the criticism and the success of others.

Criticism

Criticism does not go over very well with the fixed mindset. Fixed mindset people most often see feedback, even constructive feedback, as negative feedback. Criticism and feedback usually comes on the heels of mistakes. Mistakes are not easily tolerated by a fixed mindset. They are simply not supposed to happen to people with natural ability.

Success of Others

Fixed mindset people enjoy success. They love to see the payoff from their natural abilities. They find plenty of reasons to celebrate their own success, but rarely if ever will a fixed mindset take pleasure in the success of others. A player like Ashley with a fixed mindset is quick to get angry or defensive if a teammate receives praise, accolades, or achievements that he believes to be his.

For example, think of a high school team that includes a superstar player and surrounding role players. The superstar player is the one everyone wants to watch, the one everyone refers to as the one with natural ability. Throughout the season, the superstar has great games mingled with games in which she struggled. The team overall has experienced tremendous success, but in large part its due to one of the role players that has played consistently well all year, even helping the team win games when the superstar did not play or was not playing well. At the end of the year, the role player is awarded the team's most valuable player trophy. How does the fixed mindset superstar react? If you suggested that the superstar reacted with anger or discontent or denial, you are right. Behind that superficial handshake, the fixed mindset is steaming and looking for anyone to blame for the loss of the MVP trophy.

GROWTH MINDSET

The growth mindset believes that all aspects of our personality, intelligence, and abilities can be shaped, learned, and created to what we want them to be. Growth mindset people believe in the value of hard work and persistence, and they see tremendous value and learning in failure. Some aspects of your development certainly come naturally from genetics. Your height, build, hair color, eye color, and other physical traits are directly impacted by the genetic makeup of your parents. Let's not confuse the truly "natural" aspects of you with those that are not. The growth mindset does not break the rules of physics or genetics. It won't make you taller, much to the dislike of my own kids. Table 3.1 lists some of the characteristics that are natural versus those that can be developed. Add your own ideas to the table.

Natural Characteristics	Developed Characteristics
Height*	Strength
Wingspan	Motivation/Dedication
Standing reach	Intelligence
Eye color	Effort
Hair color	Speed/quickness
	Sportsmanship
	Communication
*Through the course of time, the average height has increased, perhaps due to proper nutrition and dietary changes, so there might be a small element of development opportunity to this characteristic.	

Table 3.1. Natural Characteristics versus Developed Characteristics. What other characteristics can you think of to add to either column?

In a growth mindset, the concept of "the natural"

seemingly still applies because that's simply how genetics tends to work out for some. But it doesn't hold as much weight because a growth mindset believes that abilities, intelligence, and personality are dynamic elements that can be shaped by our own willing determination to make purposeful change.

In 1907 psychologist William James wrote, "The plain fact remains that men the world over possess amounts of resource, which only very exceptional individuals push to their extremes of use."

If you deconstruct James's saying, you will find that though the wording certainly seems odd compared to today's writing, it doesn't make it any less true. By "men the world over," James is including all human beings in his statement. The phrase "possess amounts of resource" reflects our ability to perform, behave, move, think, speak, or put forth effort toward achievement of a goal. The last part of his statement, "which only very exceptional individuals push to their extremes of use," refers to the uniqueness of humans to not only be aware of their own innate power to do things but also to do them with consistency and intention to succeed.

Challenges

People with a growth mindset like challenges. In fact, they seek out challenges. They want to be challenged. Challenges offer growth mindsets a chance to, well, grow. Being challenged presents a chance to fail, a chance to fail presents a chance to learn, and a chance to learn is a chance to improve oneself.

As a young athlete, your academics are a key component to your development and your ability to compete in sports.

For many of you, academics in and of itself might present a challenge. Perhaps it's a specific subject or a certain teacher where you struggle. It would be easy to quickly adopt a fixed mindset and find excuses for mediocre, or even poor, performance in the classroom. Rather than blaming a teacher or suggesting your ignorance in a particular area, the growth mindset allows you to find the challenge and work toward success.

Athletes with a growth mindset are constantly looking for ways to challenge their skills against players who are better than them. Let's say you go to the local park for some pickup basketball, and there are two courts of games. Court A is made up of older players who are stronger, faster, and more skilled. Court B consists of younger kids who are still developing and learning the game. The growth mindset athlete would want to be challenged by the competition on court A. The fixed mindset athlete will be more concerned with winning and proving dominance against lesser competition on court B.

No matter what sport you play, improving your skills comes in many ways. One of those ways is being aware of your role within a game and adjusting your mindset to gain the most value. Until your body has reached its physical maturity, you will certainly find yourself in situations where the laws of physics are against you no matter how motivated you are to succeed. It's not uncommon these days to see young athletes in eighth and ninth grade playing on high school varsity sports teams. Many of these athletes have reached a physical maturity that allows them to assimilate into the situation.

We can dive deeper into this example by looking at two

athletes. Our first athlete is Nate. Nate is a ninth grader who is 6'8" and 275 pounds. For reference, at that size Nate would be right in line with the starting linemen of the 2017 New England Patriots, and he exceeds all values on growth charts available at www.cdc.gov/growthcharts. Our second athlete is TJ. TJ is a ninth grader who is 5'3" and 108 pounds. For reference, that puts TJ in the 50th percentile for fourteen-year-old boys, according to the same CDC growth chart. Let's assume that at the varsity sports level, most athletes in eleventh and twelfth grade are seventeen or eighteen years old from the 50th percentile (5'9" and 148 pounds) to the 97th percentile (6'2" and 215 pounds). If you have watched high school basketball lately, you know that rosters don't tend to match growth charts. It's likely because taller kids gravitate toward sports where height can provide a tremendous advantage.

You might have noticed that thus far I have not provided any measurements other than those that are quantifiable and measurable. Clearly, TJ has a physical disadvantage that Nate does not have because Nate is already bigger than 99 percent of existing athletes of any age. Each of these athletes has a different set of challenges in front of them as well as different roles. Even if TJ is quicker than Nate, has better cardiovascular capability than Nate, or has better skills than Nate, the situation is not TJ versus Nate—it's TJ versus the competition, and it's Nate versus the competition. Unfortunately, many kids and parents would see it as a failure if TJ was not playing at the highest level available to him (varsity), even given the size differential. If Nate and TJ share the same goal of improving as basketball players, they must look at their own situations within the context of their own characteristics.

In this situation, Nate clearly has an opportunity to get the most benefit by playing up against older kids. This is not to suggest that it would be easy for Nate. He may be at a disadvantage in speed, quickness, vertical leap, or skill. But at the very least, he is not fighting the laws of physics, and therefore his growth mindset would help him see the value in challenging himself. Playing at a lower level (without challenge or opportunity to fail) against much smaller players where he could dominate without question would hinder his long-term development.

TJ, on the other hand, has a broader scope of opportunity because there are lessons to be learned at multiple levels. TJ can find value in both junior varsity and varsity, and even more value in both. If TJ doesn't make the varsity team, his growth mindset can take on the challenge of leading a JV team knowing his skills will develop and that as time passes, he will get bigger, stronger, and faster. As a varsity player, TJ might see very limited action, thereby preventing him from getting the experience needed to help him get better in game situations. There is also a third option. TJ could take on the challenge of leading a JV team but challenge himself to be part of the varsity team, knowing that his time will be limited. With a growth mindset, TJ can challenge himself to develop an awareness of his role and capabilities as part of both a JV team and a varsity team. On the JV team, TJ might play the role of a leader, a playmaker, and a scorer; on the varsity team, his leadership and role might be more of a passer or charge taker. No matter the situation, the growth

@beast_thinking_

mindset athlete will find the value that is needed to continue moving in the direction of reaching long-term goals.

Many parents, and athletes, mistakenly feel that playing varsity at a young age is a barometer of how good you are. The reality for most kids in eighth and ninth grade is that they have not developed enough to be successful against more developed kids in the eleventh and twelfth grades. People cannot defy the laws of physics, so you should not look at this as a challenge but as an obstacle to your long-term goal. How will you respond to this insurmountable obstacle called the laws of physics? Will you be hindered by it? Will you use it to be even more motivated? Let's talk about obstacles.

Obstacles

When it comes to obstacles, none are too big or too small for a growth mindset. Persistence is a key trait for the growth mindset. New challenges and obstacles, no matter the size, are taken on as opportunities to learn and grow from failed attempts. As in TJ's case, not yet possessing the physical attributes to allow him to compete at the varsity level was not a failure to accept a challenge but rather was presented as an obstacle to overcome. There is a big difference between applying a label (failure) versus engaging in an action (failed). Which do you think a fixed mindset would do or say? There is a commonly used quote from Michael Jordan related to this very topic.

> "I've missed more than 9000 shots in my career. I've lost almost 300 games. 26 times, I've been trusted to take the game winning shot

and missed. I've failed over and over and over again in my life. And that is why I succeed."

Notice in his quote Michael says "I've failed" rather than "I'm a failure" or "I was a failure." This is Michael being a growth mindset athlete.

Perhaps the most famous example told time and time again is of Michael Jordan being cut from his high school varsity basketball team when he was a sophomore. Given what we know of Michael from his time in the NBA, it is shocking to think that anyone could have cut him from a team. When we look upon athletes as the greatest of all time, we often want to equate that with natural talent. But the reality is that Michael was one of the ultimate growth mindset athletes, even going all the way back to his days in high school. He dared himself to overcome obstacles that stood in the way of his success.

Effort

For the growth mindset, effort and persistence are weapons to be used against challenges and obstacles. Challenges and obstacles are nothing to a growth mindset because of the impact of effort. A growth mindset believes that persistent effort is the path to success. Through effort, you can master and accomplish anything. The sticking point here is in the amount of effort required. There is no quantifiable number that can be applied to effort that will suggest a specific result. Popular author Malcolm Gladwell, in his book *Outliers*, wrote that achieving world-class mastery requires that one must put in ten thousand hours of work. Gladwell's theory has since been disproven, which only shows the difficulty in trying to quantify the amount of effort required to achieve something. More on this to come in chapter 5.

Can we measure effort? Yes, absolutely. You can track the number of hours you train, study, meditate, learn, and more. But you cannot attach a training goal at which point you can state, "I cannot be better."

As humans have evolved in areas of education, arts, sports, and business, the factors determining success have also evolved beyond just physical action. For example, imagine you did spend ten thousand hours perfecting some task: shooting a basketball, hitting a baseball, serving a volleyball, playing an instrument, or studying a topic. Is there a point at which you cannot become any better? Are athletic, artistic, and academic abilities finite entities? It is not uncommon for people to use the term *mastery* to refer to someone's elite ability, but even mastery across subjects doesn't seem to have a clearly defined threshold.

mastery

noun

1. Comprehensive knowledge or skill in a subject or accomplishment
   Synonyms: proficiency, ability, capability

Now, more than ever, the mind is playing a huge role in a person's ability to achieve mastery.

MIND + BODY = MAXIMUM RESULT

Recent science has shown that we can manipulate and stimulate the brain to maximize effort. A California-based company named Halo Neuroscience makes a specialized pair of headphones, called Halo Sport, that can prime the brain for muscle memory. At first glance, the device looks like a normal pair of headphones, but then you notice the multitude of silicon nodes across the inside of the ear-to-ear band. These nodes are part of the science that Halo calls neural priming. Do you remember our discussion on neurons in the brain from chapter 2? Remember how neurons fire throughout the brain to coordinate muscle movement? Neural priming increases the brain's plasticity, or ability to optimize neural connections when performing behaviors. Here is an excerpt from their website (www.haloneuro.com) that briefly explains the importance of hyperplasticity while training or practicing.

> Halo Sport is designed to make your training or practice more efficient by improving your brain's natural plasticity. By applying a mild electric field to the motor cortex, Halo's Neuropriming technology induces a state of "hyperplasticity." When you train in a hyperplastic state, the brain's normal fine-tuning process occurs more rapidly—meaning better results from each practice rep.

Does the Halo sport really work? Does it make effort worth more? Neuroplasticity has certainly been proven true, and the science of how the brain works seems to suggest it could make a difference, but ultimately it still doesn't work without maximum effort on the part of the athlete.

Back in chapter 1, you were presented with four models that represent the culmination of sports skill, physical fitness, and mindset. What we neglected to introduce in those models is the impact of effort. Now that we have discussed the importance of effort, let's revisit those models, or perhaps a custom model you might have created, and add the element of effort. Review the four models in Figure 3.1 below and think about how you might alter each model or create one of your own.

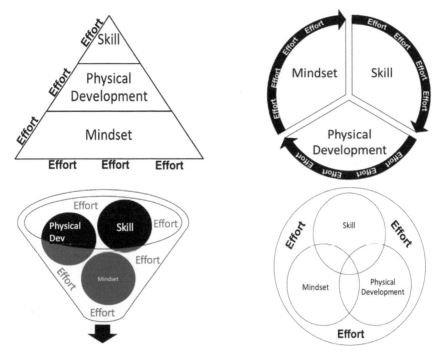

Figure 3.1. Skill, physical development,
and mindset models with effort.

In her book *Grit*, Angela Duckworth makes an extremely compelling case for the value of effort. Duckworth defines two simple formulas that identify the power of effort.

Talent × Effort = Skill

Skill × Effort = Achievement

According to Duckworth, talent is how quickly your skills improve when you apply effort, and achievement is what happens when you apply your skills. Notice though that in both equations, there is an element of effort that increases the results of talent or skill.

Let's apply some numbers to these formulas to see how they work. Imagine that talent level resides on a scale from one to ten, effort resides on a scale from one to one hundred, and they are applied in the following manner.

A talented athlete (8) applied a mediocre effort (35). Using the formula talent × effort = skill results in 8 × 35 = 280. On the other hand, a mediocre talent (4) applies an above average effort (80), which results in 4 × 80 = 320. In simple math terms, you can see that the second athlete will have a greater skill over time than the first athlete, 280 versus 320. But now take that same skill level and apply effort once again. For the first athlete with a skill rating of 280 and same effort level (35), the achievement rating will be 280 × 35, or 9,800. In the case of the second athlete with a skill rating of 320 and same effort level (80), the achievement rating will be 320 × 80, or 25,600.

Although these number don't have a specific unit value and talent can't be easily quantified, the example shows that there is a certain truth in the saying "Hard work beats talent when talent won't work hard." We just proved it mathematically.

Those actions you perform in practice, in isolation, are not the definition of success for their respective sport or subject.

In other words, success in basketball is not defined by how you shoot when alone in a gym; rather it's how you perform in games and specifically in pressure situations. Success in baseball is determined by your ability to hit when being pitched to, not while standing in a batting cage. Success in volleyball is defined by serving successfully in competition. Success in school is reflected in mastery through assessment or presentation. When you step outside the realm of practice and add to it the element of competition, there are new factors that impact the chances of success. One of those factors—a major factor that is getting a lot of attention these days—is the human mind.

That's why books like this one are a great tool for helping you understand and reach maximum potential. As much as you must learn how to perform physically, you must learn how to control yourself mentally and emotionally. To do that, you must educate yourself on how the mind, brain, and body interact and give you the tools you need to be motivated and put forth maximum effort.

Effort is a key ingredient to not only the development of your beast mind but also the achievement of your goals.

CRITICISM

What happens when effort, even optimized and maximum effort, results in failure and subsequent criticism? As we have established, when growth mindset people fail, they are looking to gain value from it. This value can come in the form of self-discovery, or it can come in the form of criticism and feedback. Unlike the fixed mindset, growth mindsets want feedback, especially constructive feedback that can potentially speed the path to success. This is a tough concept to embrace because criticism can sometimes bring to light harsh realities. Growth mindsets will persist through failure; fixed mindsets will quit easily and find excuses for doing so.

In 2009, the Golden State Warriors used their seventh pick of the NBA draft to select Stephen Curry. At the time, selecting Steph with the seventh pick had many scouts and experts scratching their heads and wondering what the Warriors were thinking. Steph had surely made some heads turn with a Cinderella-like story, taking his Davidson team deep into the 2009 NCAA tournament, but the scouts were not sold. In fact, the scouting report on Steph came across as a harsh criticism that could certainly have served a striking blow to the ego of any fixed mindset athlete. Here are some of the bullet points from Steph's NBA scouting report.

- Stephen's explosiveness and athleticism are below standard.
- He's not a great finisher around the basket.
- He needs to considerably improve his ball handling.
- He often struggles against physical defenders.
- Stephen must develop as a point guard to make it in the league.
- He will have limited success at the next level.
- Do not rely on him to run your team.

Thankfully for the NBA, basketball lovers, and Warriors fans, Steph is a growth mindset athlete. The last three years, as Steph has dominated the NBA landscape and altered the game, those scouts have had to eat their words. They never counted on the power of the growth mindset within Steph. They never expected that a growth mindset could take criticism and use it to fuel two Most Valuable Player trophies, two world championships, and a legion of players who aspire to be everything he is. Hopefully books like this will give future athletes the tools they need to develop the Steph Curry growth mindset while developing the long-range jump shot or incredible ball-handling skills. For a growth mindset athlete, getting information like this creates a blueprint for change. This blueprint plus the motivation, dedication, and determination to find success only clarifies the goal and the road to achieving it.

SUCCESS OF OTHERS

Growth mindset people are not put off by the success of others. In fact, growth mindset people learn from the success of others every bit as much as they learn from their own successes (and failures). They will celebrate the success of their friends, family, teammates, and even competitors.

Mindsets Summary

Table 3.1 provides a summary of the two mindsets. Read through the table and think about additional examples of how, where and when the mindsets can impact your situations.

	Fixed Mindset	Growth Mindset	Example Situation
Core Definition	Intelligence, abilities, outcomes, personality and character are fixed	Intelligence, abilities, outcomes, personality and character are developed	
Situational response	Will I succeed or fail? Will I look smart or dumb? Will I bee a winner or a loser? Will something negative come from it?	Will this help me get better? Will I learn something? Can I make something positive from it?	Trying something new
Failure response	I AM A FAILURE, My ___ is TRASH, I am dumb, I am no good at ___	I failed, How can I improve for next time? I am a great ___	Sports practice
Challenge response	Avoidance, defensive, quick to give up	Embrace, persist	New drill, exercise, idea or subject
Effort response	"effort doesn't change anything"	"improvement and success require effort"	Academics, improving weaknesses
Criticism response	Ignore feedback, get defensive	Seeks out criticism as a way of learning	Post-game discussions, evaluations, grades
Success response	Threatened by success of others, over indulges in personal success	Sees value and learning in personal, shared and observed success	Team sports, goal setting
Result	Premature plateau, inability to reach full potential	Reach higher levels of achievement through lifelong learning and growth	

@beast_thinking_

DEVELOPING A GROWTH MINDSET

As you already know, and probably expected, a growth mindset is something that can be developed. The way that you would develop better free throws, penalty

Life is only as good as your mindset.

kicks, pitching, or field goals is the same way that you develop a growth mindset: practice.

The growth mindset is a choice you make in your logical mind that then drives the physical brain to guide behaviors. You have already learned in this chapter that a growth mindset accepts challenges, overcomes obstacles, values effort, welcomes feedback, and finds value in the success of others. To develop a growth mindset, you can't sit around and wait for challenges, obstacles, and feedback. You must not only find opportunities, but also create opportunities.

Creating opportunities to develop a growth mindset begins with setting goals and defining all aspects of achieving those goals. Grab a notebook or some paper, explore the questions below, and think of answers.

- What is a goal I want to accomplish in the next six months? (Pick something small to start with.)
- What are the challenges I must overcome?
- What are the obstacles I will face?
- How can I track my progress toward this goal?
- What are the things (behaviors, tasks, exercises) I need to do? How often will I do them?

- Do I know someone who has done what I am trying to do, or is there someone I know who wants to achieve the same goal? Who can I use as a role model, guide, or coach?

These six questions are a starting point for helping yourself develop a growth mindset. By thinking of the answers to these questions—and writing them down—you are creating an opportunity for self-awareness. Your awareness of the challenges and obstacles is going to make you better prepared to face them and overcome them. Don't be surprised if your answers to these questions don't cover every challenge and obstacle. There are likely going to be things you didn't think of, but your momentum of overcoming the ones you did think of are going to develop your super power growth mindset.

This goal discovery exercise should be done for both short-term and long-term goals. Importantly, be realistic with your answers. The loftier your goals, the more challenges and obstacles you are sure to face. The loftier the goals, the more effort and feedback you will need. It is okay to create high level goals, but don't make them seem easy to attain. Be honest with your planning. Seek help with getting the answers you need. Most important, don't be afraid to fail. We will cover failure in the next chapter. The task of setting, working toward, and achieving goals is not a linear task, meaning it doesn't get to a point (fail or succeed) and then stop. Goal seeking, as shown in figure 3.2, is a cyclical task.

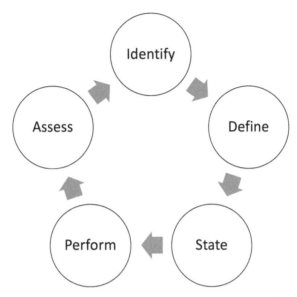

Figure 3.2. Goal seeking is a cyclical process. You will constantly revisit existing goals, as well as seek to achieve new goals.

1. Identify your goal
   a. What is it I want to accomplish?
   b. What is the target date for my goal?
2. Define success criteria
   a. What does it mean to achieve my goal?
   b. What does it look like to be successful?
3. State your intended actions to reach goal
   a. What behaviors will I do to reach my goal?
   b. What actions will I take to reach my goal?
   c. How often will I perform the behaviors and actions?
4. Perform
   a. Just do it!
5. Assess
   a. Did I reach my goal?

b. If I didn't reach my goal, why?

c. Was the goal set too high?

d. Were the success criteria not clearly defined?

e. Were my intended actions incomplete or insufficient?

f. Did I perform as often as I could or as needed to achieve my goal?

As you work on developing your growth mindset, understand that your words and responses will be key factors in success. Figure 3.3 lists responses that differentiate the growth mindset versus the fixed mindset.

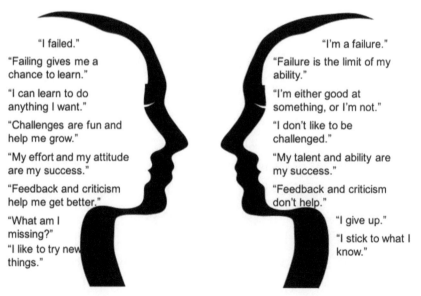

"I failed."

"Failing gives me a chance to learn."

"I can learn to do anything I want."

"Challenges are fun and help me grow."

"My effort and my attitude are my success."

"Feedback and criticism help me get better."

"What am I missing?"

"I like to try new things."

"I'm a failure."

"Failure is the limit of my ability."

"I'm either good at something, or I'm not."

"I don't like to be challenged."

"My talent and ability are my success."

"Feedback and criticism don't help."

"I give up."

"I stick to what I know."

Figure 3.3. Common responses of the growth mindset and fixed mindset.

If you dedicate yourself to the art and science of developing a growth mindset, there is no doubt you will see change in your life.

CHAPTER 4
Emotions

C AN YOU THINK about what it means to love someone or something? Or even the opposite, what does it mean to hate someone or something? When you think about these powerful emotions, what comes to mind as representations of these polar opposite words? If you are like most people, you might be stumped at finding the right words to describe exactly what you are thinking—or more to the point, feeling—when you think of these emotions.

You can't touch emotions.

You can't see emotions.

You can't feel emotions.

It's interesting that some of life's most powerful moments are described by words that are themselves difficult to describe. Emotions are labels that we give to physical responses or actions taken in response to some external stimuli or experience. Interestingly, the physical responses that occur during love and hate often overlap: increased heartbeat, sweating, tension in the stomach. But then again, those same responses can be applied to other emotions like anxiety, excitement, nervousness, and happiness. How, then, can emotions be labels to these physical responses? The answer is that we have to apply context to the feelings to determine the right label to apply.

As a kid, you wake up on Christmas morning, and you're excited to see what the day brings. As soon as you wake up, your heart is probably beating a little faster, a smile appears on your face, and there is a tingle in your stomach. Walking into a room of unknown goodness on Christmas morning is the context that allows your mind to define your emotion as excited or happy.

Now apply a different context. Maybe today is report card day, you didn't quite put forth the best effort, and your grades reflect that lack of effort. Greeting your waiting parents with this report card has your heart beating a little faster, a frown upon your face, and your stomach in a knot. Walking into a situation of potential anger on report card day is the context that allows your mind to define your emotion as nervous or scared.

These are two completely different situations with most of the same physical responses, yet they're perceived and defined by our minds in two different ways.

Emotions might also be described as actions we would or would not take. A parent who loves her child makes sacrifices for that child. A child who hates a food will avoid eating that food. These actions, or lack of actions, are decisions made by the conscious mind. The decisions allow us to reaffirm our label toward a person, place, or thing.

Although emotions are often reactions to events in

our lives using our minds, we can learn to be proactive in controlling our emotions. This certainly isn't always easy considering the power of events that cause strong emotions. Controlling our emotions often involves figuring out how to use the mind to control the physical responses we are having and apply an emotional label.

In the book *Super Brain,* authors Chopra and Tanzi mention that the limbic system is the center for emotion. But if emotions exist only in name, how can there be a place from which emotion originates? Further research has shown that the limbic system is not just a center for emotion but is also involved in motivation, learning, memory, and smell. Chapter 2 introduced you to the major regions of the brain and briefly dipped into how anatomically complex, efficient, and powerful the brain can be. I am going to spare you the anatomy of the limbic system, but within that complex brain is a limbic system that is so complex it is made up of twelve different parts. Then again, would you expect a simple structure to handle such critical aspects as motivation, learning, memory, and smell? (If you want the details on the limbic system, you can google it.)

The limbic system is not unique to humans. There are animals that also have limbic systems. Does this mean that animals have emotions? Well, they certainly have physical responses to external stimuli, but their inability to speak prevents them from assigning a label to it—though we as humans have no problems doing that. Animals most certainly use their limbic system for the sense of smell because most have more powerful smell senses than humans. Does a dog feel sad? Does a dog feel happy? We'll never really know what they call it, but you can certainly scour YouTube and find videos of dogs that clearly show physical symptoms of happy and excited. Similarly, you can find other dogs that show physical symptoms of being sad, nervous, and scared. But remember, that is me applying those labels. The dog is none the wiser to the label.

We could write hundreds of pages just on human emotion, as others have, but for our purposes, we are going to focus on two specific emotions: fear and happiness.

FEAR

Fear is, and has been, a commonly studied emotion. Among the many books on fear, you will find that most, if not all, acknowledge fear as a natural part of being human. Also common among these books is the notion that fear is something that we can overcome by understanding how to use our minds to overpower situations that draw us to being fearful.

The most natural and understandable feeling of fear is that which comes as fear of death to yourself or to someone you care for deeply. If for any reason you are in a position where you are currently in fear for your life or the life of someone close to you, I suggest that you stop reading and seek immediate help and guidance. This book is not about overcoming the natural fear of death, though that fear can be overcome even in dire circumstances.

If you think about the earliest times of modern humans, it will help you to understand both the natural and the evolved misconceptions of fear. From there, we will discuss how to become a more powerful champion over your fears.

Many thousands of years ago, the earliest humans were required to hunt and gather their own food. These tasks were not without risk. Being out in the wild with other predators and environmental dangers posed significant risk to the lives of early humans. Without the hunt, it was likely that families would starve and die. They had to hunt for their survival while knowing that hunting could be the cause of their death. In this example, you should be able to understand how they feared the hunting and gathering process but at the same time knew it to be necessary for their survival. The desire to live for a longer period of time was stronger than the instinct to avoid situations that may cause death. We are no longer living in a society where we must hunt for our food and put ourselves at risk of death to get something to eat. We have, in fact, evolved.

Just as our society, tools, industries, science, transportation, communication, medicine, technologies, and people have evolved, so too have our minds and brains. In some ways, this evolution has been great for our world. But this evolution has also had a fair share of negative impact. Most relevant to this part of the book is the evolution of the fear emotion that humans have.

As I mentioned a few paragraphs ago, we no longer live in a world where we must hunt for our food. We no longer live in a time where our lives are in constant jeopardy just to obtain vitals for living. However, fear is extremely prevalent in today's world for people of all ages. These fears are rooted in a variety of things.

Thankfully, most of the fears today are self-imposed fears

that are rooted in self-imposed misconceptions of our own abilities. If you think hard about the concept of fear, you should find that fears are inspired by the potential outcome of an action, not the action itself. The three most common fears in humans are the fear of spiders (arachnophobia), the fear of snakes (ophidiophobia), and the fear of heights (acrophobia). In all three of these cases, it likely that people fear the outcome of the stimulus rather than the stimulus itself. People fear being bit by spiders and snakes or falling from heights more than the actual spiders, snakes, or tall places. Fear of public speaking is another popular fear. Do you think people fear having to speak, or do you think they fear the outcome or response from the people to whom they are speaking? Speaking to one person comes with very little risk of rejection or dislike unless you are speaking to a stranger—and some people do, in fact, fear strangers. Speaking to one hundred or one thousand people comes with one hundred or one thousand times more risk of rejection or dislike, which is the root of the fear of public speaking. In these cases, the individual is already deciding an outcome before the event even happens. The mind is generating premature fear.

In his book *The Motivation Manifesto,* author Brandon Bouchard states that fear is "a mental construct that we alone fuel with small thoughts that betray our magnitude."

Once more: Fear is a mental construct that we alone fuel with small thoughts that betray our magnitude.

A "mental construct" means that we create a situation of fear where it need not exist. Barring extreme circumstances, the fears you have in your daily life with respect to sports, school, relationships, or work are not situations that require you to be fearful.

"Small thoughts" is a reference to the inability to think bigger, to think about the relative insignificance of a single event in the big picture of our lives. In fear-driven situations, we often lose the ability to think and process information in a rational way. The fight-or-flight response is a physiological reaction that happens because of a real or perceived threat. Imagine that you are among a group of early humans from thousands of years ago. While hunting for food, you come face-to-face with an apex predator. The body will release hormones that will stimulate neural activity, which will result in either fighting the predator or fleeing from the predator. In this situation, it seems appropriate that this occurs. This is the same thing that happens in today's non-life-threatening situations like free throws in the final seconds of the game, the last at bat to bring in a victory, giving a speech, or taking a test. Clearly, you are not going to fight your opponent or the teacher, and neither are you going to run out of the gym, off the field, or out of the classroom. However, the physiological activity in the brain is the same. Hormones stimulate neural activity that causes you to respond in a fight-or-flight response. You can step up and knock down the free throws. You can step up and swing for the fences. You can step up and deliver the speech. You can sit down, focus, and pass that test. Alternatively, you can let the flight response take you mentally out of having the physical ability to complete the actions needed to become victorious.

The phrase "betray our magnitude" in Bouchard's

statement refers to the fact that by allowing our small thoughts to fuel fear, we are negating the reality that we have the power to overcome a perceived fear and move past it in a successful way.

Back in chapter 2, I introduced a scenario that involved jumping on to a box. As an athlete, you likely participate in strength and conditioning programs. If so, you have certainly come across an exercise known as box jumps. In this exercise, as the name suggests, you jump from the ground onto a box. Even though the principle is simple, the exercise can be looked at as a complex set of movements both for getting up on to the box as well as landing on the box. The exercise can be modified for a single foot, two feet, vertical jump, lateral jump, and more. Ultimately, every athlete defines the difficulty of this exercise by the height of the box. Obviously the taller the box gets, the more difficult the chance of success becomes.

Assume that you were asked to jump up on to the box and that after each successful jump the box would be raised. It could be raised a half an inch or a full inch; the amount is not important. As noted in chapter 2, there are two things that will eventually happen: you will think you cannot make the jump, or you won't be able to make the jump. The important consideration here is which will come first.

The first event, where you think you cannot make the jump, is a fear-based limitation. This is extremely common among athletes, students, artists, musicians, teachers, parents, business people, and other humans. Fear-based limitations are self-imposed and are very damaging to our mindset. As this chapter has discussed, the fear in this case is not the fear of jumping but the fear of not making it on to the box. These fears are very powerful deterrents to success. Allowing these types of fears to dictate behavior is the very opposite of having a growth mindset. If you don't believe that you can jump onto the box, even if the height is low enough to physically allow you to do so, your mind is fueling an illusionary fear that can and likely will communicate to the body that same inability, which will then result in the self-fulfilling prophecy of you not being successful.

In her book *Feel the Fear and Do It Anyway*, Susan Jeffers refers to this type of fear as a level 2 fear. Jeffers defines a level 2 fear as one that is reflective of an inner state of mind, not an exterior situation. She includes all of the following as level 2 fears.

- Rejection
- Success
- Helplessness
- Failure
- Disapproval
- Vulnerability

In 2017, I saw a video of Will Smith discussing a particularly fearful situation he had gotten himself into. In his story, he had "man-talked" his way into going skydiving with friends. Now, clearly this is a situation where fear can be extremely intense because there is some degree of chance that death or injury can occur. Smith tell of this fear hounding him the entire night before his jump. This fear intensifies during the morning as the jump time nears and the plane begins its ascent. The door opens, and the countdown starts. One. Two. Falling. This is the point where you would expect there to be the most intense feeling of fear, but instead you find that the moment is perfect happiness. Smith said, "You realize at the point of maximum danger is the point of minimum fear … it's pure bliss … everything leading up to the stepping out point … there's actually no reason to be scared … the best things in life are on the other side of your maximum fear." Figure 4.1 shows a representation of the idea that on the other side of your maximum fear is a range of contradicting emotions. Can you think of more emotions to add to the list on the right?

Figure 4.1. On the other side of your maximum fear is a range of contradicting emotions.

Think of this story from the perspective of an athlete. It's not a skydiving appointment you have tomorrow but a big game. It's a rival game, a state championship, or perhaps a game where college coaches will be watching. Leading up to the game, you are feeling those same feelings that Smith talks about. The big difference is that your situation lacks the possibility of death, but the thought process, the physical reactions, and the mindset are still the same. Just as in Smith's story, fear is a pointless emotion because when you get to take that game-winning shot or step up to the plate for the final at bat, those moments are the pinnacle of athletic success. Those are the moments that few people get to understand. They are the moments for which you strive. Why else would you put in the work? Why else would you spend so many hours conditioning your body to respond the right way? Those moments are bliss, but only if your mind allows you to interpret the situation for its uniqueness, and only if your mind finds the opportunity for growth.

The mind is engineered to prevent you from doing things you fear, as well as anything that might hurt you, might make you feel uncomfortable, or is perceived as difficult. Our minds are designed to provide protection from these things. But all of this is overcome with the mind's ability to make decisions to the contrary. By understanding the source of fear and knowing that fear is created from our own interpretation of events that have yet to occur, we can develop and evolve into conscious-driven human beings with the ability to not only face life's biggest challenges but also welcome them. In the case of a last-second shot, final at bat, or game-winning serve, you do not fear the event itself—you fear the outcome of the event. Yet you don't even know the outcome, and thus your fear is an interpretation of an event that has yet to happen. The pending shot, swing, or serve is very real, but the outcome has yet to be decided. Letting fear consume you to the point that it impedes your abilities creates a greater chance that your feared interpretation becomes a reality. Overcoming fears and finding perfect happiness in the face of maximum fear is possible when you adopt a growth mindset rooted in the confidence of your own mental and physical abilities.

HAPPINESS

Happiness, unlike fear, has not been studied for as long. In fact, it wasn't until recently that scientists began to do studies on happiness. In his book *The Happiness Advantage*, Shawn Achor provides in-depth data from studies performed in the areas of positive psychology and neuroscience. Achor's book provides overwhelming scientific proof that contradicts the long-standing idea that success breeds happiness. Studies show that the relationship is actually the other way around: happiness breeds success. To put it quite simply, the people who are found to be happy are the same people who experience the most success. And I mean true happiness; I am not referring to smile emojis and LOLs sent via text.

Understanding this concept is a critical attribute for athletes who want to maximize their abilities in a competitive environment. This is a critical attribute for all people to understand across different aspects of life, work, education, friends, family, athletics, and self-awareness. We are focused on young athletes, so we will look at it from an athletic perspective.

Most, if not all athletes, begin their athletic careers with the simple notion that winning a championship in their sport is what will make them happy, because championships are most often used as the defining factor for athletes' arrival at the pinnacle of success. There are many athletes whose careers, at first glance, can seem to support the idea that success comes before happiness—think Michael Jordan. But if you look a little more closely at Michael's career in the NBA, you will find that he was drafted in 1984 and didn't win his first championship until 1991. Are you willing to argue that Michael was unhappy with himself for seven years straight? That is a fixed mindset and old-school thinking. Elite-level and growth mindset athletes might use championships as a barometer for success, but not as the definition of happiness. They might use championships to measure their success versus other athletes, but they don't use championships in their own personal definitions of success (and happiness). The same thing can be said for athletes of other sports, as well as all the best students, scientists, and businesspeople.

Kobe Bryant is arguably one of the best to ever play in the NBA, but he is inarguably one of the best competitors to ever play the game. To the casual fan, he was a dominant force, a boy turned man who not only won five world championships but also led his team in each victorious season. Very few professional athletes have been as outspoken about the mental side of athletics as Kobe. In 2015, Kobe did a television interview with Ahmad Rashad. That year was one of the last of his career, and it was a year where he spent a lot of time recovering from injury. It allowed Kobe to reflect and provide perspective on his career because he knew it was winding down. The text that follows is bits and pieces from the interview and a breakdown of the mindset that made his words and actions so powerful.

Ahmad Rashad (on Kobe's rehabilitation): And never one day was it like, Ugh, it's too much?

Kobe Bryant: Yeah, of course. Of course. When I had those moments, I always realized I was having those moments when I was looking at the big picture. Looking at the finish line. Then you kind of check yourself. Don't worry about that. Say okay. Focus on now. That's a constant dance. Happens all the time. Happens for me now.

Kobe's answer shows just how important it was for him to know that his happiness was not defined by the bigger picture but by loving the moment he was in and finding happiness in the now. Interestingly, his response also shows that even the ones we see as the greatest, the ones we think are so natural, have moments where they too have to be conscious of their mindset; they even have to reset their minds and the flow of their thoughts.

This is a very powerful statement coming from one of the most elite athletes and champions in the history of his sport. If he needed these moments of reset, it goes without saying that as a teenager, you will most certainly need them. Perhaps you need them more often. For Kobe, he was able to identify when he needed to refocus and redefine. For you, it may not be as easy to identify those moments. As a teenager, it is advantageous to regularly be self-aware. To use Kobe's words, you need to "check yourself." Regularly ask yourself these questions.

- Are you happy?
- Are you focused on the now with a strategic vision of your goals?

Ahmad Rashad: What drives you to come back?

Kobe Bryant: The process of it. I want to see if I can … I am going to do what I always do. Just break everything down to its smallest form, the smallest detail, and go after it. Day by day, just one day at a time … I do what I have to do.

As you read this, I hope that you were able to quickly identify the growth-minded nature of the response. But not only does this suggest the growth-minded genius of Kobe Bryant, it also shows that he was able to control the highly emotional impact of being injured and having to see the upcoming nine months of rehabilitation he would have to endure. By saying "I want to see if I can," Kobe is embracing the challenge ahead of him. A fixed mindset would have felt overwhelmed at back-to-back years of rehabilitating injuries. Kobe took them head-on.

Although frustration and disappointment are expected and understood for any athlete who becomes injured, Kobe seems to have found happiness in the challenge of making it back to his normal form. His ability to "break everything down to its smallest form" allowed him to remain focused on the day-to-day. He could then find happiness in the small progressions he made.

Kobe Bryant (on his December 17, 1997, game versus Michael Jordan and the Chicago Bulls): This was a fun game for me. I learned a lot this game. A lot about how technically sound

Michael was … his technique was flawless. I wanted to make sure my technique was just as flawless. That was very inspiring for me.

Think of your favorite player in the sport you play. Imagine yourself playing against the person in a game at the highest level of your sport. How would you react? Would you be nervous? Scared? Excited? Passive? Aggressive? For Kobe, the game was fun. From his response, you can certainly understand that playing against Michael was not just fun but also a chance for him to learn. It was a chance for him to get better in a single instant. Michael's success wasn't a point of contention for Kobe, rather Kobe's growth mindset allowed him to be happy for Michael. Kobe was only envious of Michael's success in a manner that drove him to achieve similar success, not in a manner that breeded negativity. His mindset wasn't focused on the outcome of potentially being beaten by Michael; instead, he was focused on understanding Michael and learning from him so that he could grow as a player. You can hear in Kobe's voice the admiration he had for Michael's skills. You can hear the determination in his voice and the confidence that he knew on that day that he would happily work every day to have that same flawless technique. And it's hard to argue that he didn't.

For the record, the Bulls beat the Lakers, 104–83.

Later in the interview, Ahmad Rashad tells a story of a twenty-one-year-old Kobe years after his first game with MJ, when Phil Jackson was the coach of the Lakers. Kobe went beyond wanting to learn from Michael—he actually challenged MJ to come out to a Lakers practice and play one-on-one. Clearly there was no challenge Kobe wouldn't take on, and he founded his happiness on that passion.

> Kobe Bryant (on his work ethic): Basketball never felt like work to me. Once I came to the NBA and I looked around, I saw all the other guys that weren't working as much as I was, and I started to understand that how I went about it was "hard work." To me, it was just, I love what I do, so I want to do it as much as possible.

If you haven't yet begun to understand that Kobe's definition of happiness was formed in the details of his everyday life, then reread the quote above. This is perhaps the most powerful quote from Kobe that will help you understand the importance of finding happiness in the day-to-day processes of becoming great. When you love what you do, and when you are happy in the small details, then those things don't feel like work. Redefine your happiness to center on the things you can do day-to-day, and your success will follow. The science shows it, and so does the anecdotal evidence in Kobe Bryant.

> Ahmad Rashad: Did you set goals when you started in the NBA? Did you have goals at that point?
>
> Kobe Bryant: Yeah, it was really simple for me at the time: win as many championships as possible. That was it. Growing up, I understood that to be the standard. I watched Magic

[Johnson] win five. I watched Michael [Jordan] win six.

Earlier, this chapter mentioned that many athletes define their success by championships. Kobe was not different here. Early in his career, he set a goal to win as many championships as he could. As noted, it was his barometer by which he could compare himself to the other great NBA players like Ervin "Magic" Johnson and Michael Jordan. It is important, though, to know the difference between setting goals and defining happiness. These are not the same thing, and neither are they mutually exclusive from one another. They are, in fact, intertwined. From the few excerpts published earlier, you can get a picture that Kobe was in love with the process of becoming great, and he found happiness in the details that others considered hard work.

The mindset of finding happiness is not unique to Kobe Bryant, and neither is it unique to basketball. There are ample stories from other athletes like Ray Allen, Jerry Rice, and Venus and Serena Williams, just as there are stories about successful businesspeople like Bill Gates and Steve Jobs. The uniqueness is not in the people but in the mindset that happiness is not derived from an end result but from the process that happens along the way. Happiness breeds success, not the other way around.

If your happiness is attached to the outcome of an event or the attainment of a goal, you run the dangerous risk of becoming a victim to your own success. This is especially true of highly motivated, success-driven people. If you are the type of person I mentioned and you define happiness by attaining a goal, then the chances of you being happy are slim to none. Here is why.

Imagine you set a goal; it might be money, fame, or a championship. You know that you will be happy when you finally reach that goal. How could you not? You work every day toward it. You sacrifice for it. It is all you can think about. You want it so badly. You are driven. You are motivated. You fight the battles that need fighting. You give every bit of effort you can at whatever expense you can. And then … finally, success.

But here is where the problem begins, because as a highly motivated, superdetermined individual, you won't rest on that success. It won't be long before you now ask yourself, "What next?" This vicious cycle will continue again and again as you rack up successes, but your happiness will be short-lived. Your happiness will exist only from the time you finish one success until the time you define your next. This is not to suggest that goals are in any way a negative factor; the point is that your happiness should not be defined solely by the outcome. Find happiness in what it takes to get there, and you will be more likely to get there. In the event that you don't get there or have to make adjustments, you have not wasted time being unhappy.

The physiological and psychological constructs of happiness are impacted by time and activity. Spending more time doing things that make you happy instead of things that don't make you happy has a positive impact on your physical and mental health. Above-average levels of happiness can also fade over time. A person who lives by success-driven happiness will, over time, spend less time as a happy person than a person who lives by process-driven happiness. Take a look at figure 4.2 below.

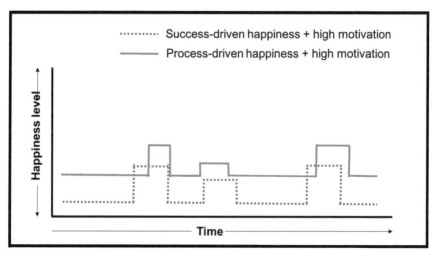

Figure 4.2. Success-driven happiness
versus process-driven happiness.

Figure 4.2 compares success-driven happiness versus process-driven happiness. The figure shows the level of happiness over a period of time for the two different mindsets. Each increase in happiness assumes that a success event has occurred. Overall, you can see that the success-driven happiness spends a greater period of time at a higher level of happiness. Let's take a deeper look at what the chart is showing, but let's also look at some of the assumptions and potential changes.

The chart assumes that tasks that take a longer period of time to achieve results in a higher level of happiness. Although this seems like a natural assumption, it is not always true. You might set a goal that is very personal for you that is accomplished in a short period of time and that results in a higher level of happiness than a separate goal that took a longer period of time to achieve; this is shown in figure 4.3. The overall happiness level of the process-driven happiness mindset is still higher than the success-driven happiness mindset.

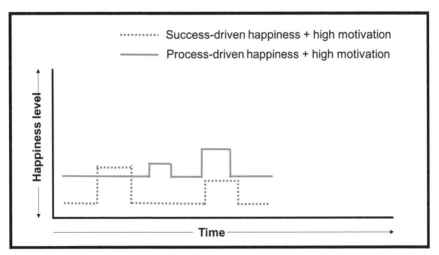

Figure 4.3. Short-term goals can result in higher levels of happiness than the success of a long-term goal in either mindset.

Figure 4.3 shows that the duration of time spent at the highest levels of happiness after success of an event is variable. It is easy to suggest that bigger moments of success will result in a longer period of post-success happiness. This isn't necessarily true, though, because folks who are process-driven may return to normal in a more rapid manner. Despite this shorter time at elevated levels of happiness, the process-driven mindset folks still have a higher level of happiness over time. This is shown in Figure 4.4.

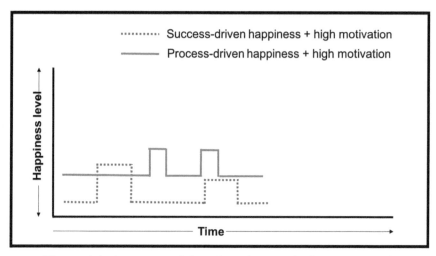

Figure 4.4. A process-driven happiness mindset may result in shorter durations of post-success happiness elevation.

Figure 4.5 shows that the increase in happiness level after success can vary. This is a result of variances in the person, the event, and the mindset. A success-driven happiness mindset might experience a tremendous increase in happiness only to have an equally tremendous return to normal. The chart also shows that process-driven happiness is always greater than success-driven happiness, which may not be the case. People with a success-driven happiness mindset might actually become happier than people with a process-driven happiness mindset. But ultimately this enhanced state of happiness does not last. This has actually been proven true in sports, education, business and even lottery winners. Everyone thinks winning the lottery will result in a lifetime of happiness. There is ample evidence to suggest that winning the lottery actually has the opposite effect, whereby winners end up more stressed and unhappy than they were prior to winning life-changing amounts of money. Figure 4.5 shows different scenarios, as described above, but once again the overall level of happiness is higher for the process-driven happiness mindset.

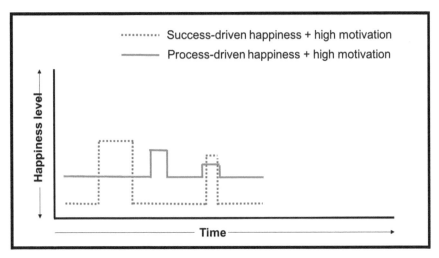

Figure 4.5. Happiness levels can vary by mindset. Success-driven happiness mindsets can experience extreme increases in happiness followed by a subsequent return to normal lows.

In November 2016, future Hall of Fame basketball player Ray Allen wrote a letter to his younger self. This letter was featured as part of an ongoing series on a website called The Players' Tribune, which was created by Derek Jeter, the New York Yankees legend. In his letter, Ray Allen sarcastically tells his pre–Jesus Shuttlesworth self the big secret to being a success in the NBA.

> The secret is there is no secret. It's just boring old habits. In every locker room you'll ever be in, everybody will *say* all the right things. Everybody says they are willing to sacrifice whatever it takes to win a title. But this game

isn't a movie. It's not about being the man in the fourth quarter. It's not about talk. It's getting in your work every single day, when nobody is watching.

Ray continues to describe how, the day after winning an NBA title with the Miami Heat in 2013, he woke and drove himself to the dentist like it was any other day. He writes, "You have achieved exactly what you set out to do. But you're still restless. So why do you feel this way? Isn't this what you worked so hard for? … This is what success looks like for you. You're the kind of guy who goes to the dentist the morning after winning an NBA title."

Though these are just a few of the excerpts from Ray Allen's full letter, there is this chilling sense of devotion you can feel from his words. His sarcastic reference to the boring habits, his jab at those who talk the talk but can't walk the walk, his downplay of fourth-quarter stardom, and his sly dig that at his own movie-star status tells you that Ray was deeply dedicated to the process of becoming great and not the ensuing limelight that came as a result of those efforts. He was certainly a superstar. His movie role became iconic. He made perhaps the greatest shot in a greatest playoff game in the history of the NBA finals to keep the Heat and LeBron James's legacy from burning. Those weren't boring habits that made Ray a Hall of Fame player; those were the moments he loved the most, and they were the process from which he derived his happiness.

Let's be clear on a very important aspect of process, happiness, and love of the process. The process to becoming great is difficult. It is filled with hard work, sweat, blood, soreness, vomit, and hopefully tears. Loving the process doesn't mean that you love vomiting when you push yourself to your limits. Loving the process doesn't mean that strength and conditioning training doesn't push your body to uncomfortable levels of pain. Loving the process means that your mindset finds success, value, and happiness from the fact that you have overcome the natural inclinations to avoid putting yourself in situations that cause such ill effects. Not everyone becomes a Kobe Bryant or Ray Allen because not everyone is willing to push oneself to extreme levels, then reflect on it with a positive attitude, and find that it truly makes one happy.

One can look at all the examples I have provided and say, "But all of those athletes are so talented." There is truth to this fixed mindset type of statement, but it does not provide the basis for their success. Just like success does not translate to happiness, talent does not translate to success. There are thousands of talented people who are not successful. On the other side of the coin, there are thousands of successful people who are not talented. Do not allow fixed mindset thinking to invade your definition of success. Do not allow fixed mindset thinking to corrupt the characteristics you use to define a successful person. The growth mindset identifies the characteristics of talented and successful people with the understanding that their uniqueness comes from their ability to harness a talent that lies within all of us. This talent is our ability to control our minds. Our minds provide the definitions and interpretations of the world around us. Our minds deliver the perspective of situations. Our minds allow us to make decisions, formulate plans, and construct happiness.

Happiness breeds success, not the other way around. Find what makes you happy. It could basketball, softball, football, science, math, real estate, broadcasting, or anything your mind can dream up. Then break it down into its smallest components and happily work to become great.

FEAR AND CHANGE

The world around us changes. I would say *evolves*, but that has a connotation that things are progressing forward, which is certainly not always the case, so let's stick with *changes*. Very little in life is static by nature, especially that which is most important. Change is a matter of fact and a factor of time. We grow out of the old and into the new, and there is nothing wrong with that, even if it means outgrowing relationships, habits, ideas, and behaviors that are detrimental to our personal happiness and success. It's okay to smoothly transition to the next phase of your life. Resisting necessary change only amplifies the complexities. You can't force people to grow, just as you can't expect all evolution to be for the greater good. It's a dangerous game to play when trying to change that which doesn't want to change. Embracing change challenges the status quo and changes the dynamic of life's interactions. No matter how uncomfortable you are, don't be afraid of the changes that you know are required to bring progress. As Brandon Bouchard puts it, "Fear was given to us as a means of preventing death or harm. It is we who have perverted it into a tool for the ego's protection." Don't fear change. Be an agent for change. At the end of the day, the ability to change is simply a choice to be made in a single instant.

CHAPTER 5
Grit and Grind

SEARCH THROUGH ANY social media platform and you will find posts about the grind. According to the Google dictionary, *grind* is defined as:

1. reduce (something) to small particles or powder by crushing it
   synonyms: crush, pound, pulverize, crumble, smash, press

2. rub or cause to run together gratingly
   synonyms: rub, grate, scrape, rasp

But in the culture of hard work, grind has taken on a new meaning. Grind is the consistent hard work it takes to achieve one's goal. Grind is the day in and day out blood, sweat, and tears that someone puts forth to improve and be great.

Grind is *crushing* the distractions.
Grind is *pounding* the court.

Grind is *pulverizing* the haters.
Grind is *crumbling* the obstacles.
Grind is *smashing* through barriers.
Grind is *pressing* on in the face of adversity.

Enjoying the grind is growth mindset. Simply put, the grind is working hard to achieve goals. Not once a month or even once a week, but every day. Grinding is performing all the behaviors needed to reach immediate and long-term goals. Grinding is sacrificing. Grinding day in and day out is much easier said than done. So what does it take to be consistent, or persistent, in your grind? It takes grit. The ability to maintain the grind is grit.

1. small, loose particles of stone or sand.
   synonyms: sand, dust, dirt

2. courage and resolve; strength of character
   synonyms: courage, bravery, pluck, mettle, backbone, spirit, strength of will, moral fiber, steel, nerve, fortitude, toughness, hardiness, resolve, resolution, determination, tenacity, perseverance, endurance

For such a small word, grit surely has huge meaning and impactful synonyms. The word *grit* is quickly gaining popularity among psychologists in large part thanks to Angela Duckworth, whose book, *Grit*, is a powerful tool for understanding the development of human behavior as it relates to our ability to maintain focus on and passion for our goals.

Beyond that, she explores the importance of practice,

but not just routine practice. She focuses on the concept of practicing with deliberate intention. She outlines four basic requirements of deliberate practice.

1. A clearly defined stretch goal
2. Full concentration and effort
3. Immediate and informative feedback
4. Repetition with reflection and refinement

If your practice is missing any of these four elements, then your time and effort is not being maximized in pursuit of something greater. Deliberate practice is separate from motivation and passion. You can be motivated and passionate but not exemplify the elements of deliberate practice.

Back in chapter 3, we showed you Angela Duckworth's formulas for skill and achievement. Here they are again as a reminder.

$$\text{Talent} \times \text{Effort} = \text{Skill}$$
$$\text{Skill} \times \text{Effort} = \text{Achievement}$$

In his book *The Talent Code*, Daniel Coyle explores deliberate practice in the form of what he calls deep practice. Deep practice is "not ordinary practice," Coyle writes; it "is something else: a highly targeted error-focused process." Deliberate, deep practice is intentional and fully aware of mistakes. Deep practice focuses on the mistakes and how to overcome them. People often mistake routine practice for being the factor behind building new skills. Perhaps for simple things, quantity of practice might be sufficient. But to develop complex skills as shown by high-level athletes, the same math does not always work out. Take a basketball player, for example. A basketball player can get to a court and shoot one thousand shots a day. Surely there will be some amount of improvement from that many shots. However, what if the goal was not to shoot one thousand shots but to *make* five hundred shots? The athlete might have a more focused approach to training in the second example. Even better, what if the goal was to make three hundred shots using perfect shooting form—knees bent, elbow in and up, ball under the hand, good release point, hold follow-through? Surely you can see how each of these varies in the amount of effort put forth physically and mentally. Shooting one thousand random shots takes more physical effort than mental effort, whereby making three hundred shots with perfect form takes less physical effort but much more mental effort. Especially when those three hundred made shots are accompanied by the awareness and correction of mistakes as shots are made and missed. In this example, the goal of making three hundred shots with good form is deep practice.

Daniel Coyle outlines three rules for deep practice.

Rule 1: Chunk it. Break down the learning into small, easy-to-repeat pieces. Coyle suggests seeing the whole and knowing the whole, but chunking it into small pieces.

Rule 2: Repeat it. This is where myelin comes into play. In chapter 2, we defined myelin as the covering of a neural pathway that speeds up transmission through the brain. What most people call muscle memory is actually myelin being built across a neural pathway as a behavior is repeated again and again.

Rule 3: Learn to feel it. There is no substitution for

repetition, but as shown in the previous example, calculated, focused, intentional repetition is better than random repetition without awareness of mistakes. In order for deep practice to be a powerful catalyst toward learning new behaviors, athletes must learn to feel mistakes and perfection. You can't feel myelin building in the brain, but you will have anecdotal evidence of improvement over the course of your training. Basketball players will notice improvements in ball handling and shooting. Volleyball players will notice improvements in setting and spiking. Piano players will notice fluency in the pieces they play. With deep practice, you can feel when something is correct and when it is not. Being able to recognize and make adjustments allows myelin to build over the proper neural pathways that create fluency in behaviors over time.

When you follow these three rules to deep practice, it will mean less thought will have to go into real performances. Kyrie Irving doesn't think about his dribble during intense moments of the game. He relies on the myelinated neural pathways that have built up over the many hours of deep practice spent with a ball bouncing under his hands.

Changing your mindset to understand and appreciate the value of effort must be coupled with goal setting, performance monitoring, and commitment to all the behaviors it takes to succeed no matter how small they

Keep your mind right, keep your grind right.

may be. Although many athletes set high-level goals, most

of them do not set measurable goals that allow for consistent checking of progress. Even fewer athletes think about all the small behaviors that together make up a huge part of reaching their goals. For example, athletes can often be heard saying, "I want to play in the pros." This is a high-level goal. This high-level goal to play in the pros is made up of many behaviors, as any high0level goal would be.

Defining a high-level goal, its subgoals, and the constructive behaviors that support those goals is the first part of developing grit. If grit is about staying the course, overcoming obstacles, having passion, and having perserverance, then you should know exactly what it is that you need to do to get you to your goal.

High-level goals should have subgoals. Those subgoals will then have supporting behaviors. Together, all these parts will create a tree of measurable, observable behaviors and outcomes. This tree will be your guide to reaching your goals. Your ability to do all the things in the tree will be the yardstick by which your grit is measured. We are going to call it the Inverted Goals and Grit (IG2) Tree.

Let's start by understanding the IG2 Tree structure, and then we can look at a specific example. As you might suspect, you're going to be responsible for building your own IG2 Tree too!

Figure 5.1 shows a simple and generic version of an IG2 Tree. The IG2 Tree begins with a single high-level goal. As you move down the tree structure, it branches out to include more details about the subgoals that support the high-level goal, followed by characterisitcs and behaviors that support the subgoals.

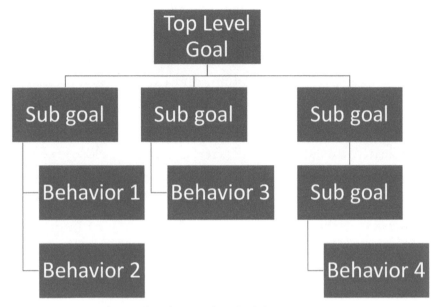

Figure 5.1. A generic IG2 Tree structure.

Figure 5.1 is a simple version of an IG2 Tree: a top-level goal, four subgoals, and four behaviors. Hopefully, you now understand the concept of the IG2 Tree. Let's add some real data and look at the beginnings of a more specific, larger, and growing IG2 Tree. Figure 5.2 shows the start of an IG2 Tree for a young athlete who sets a top-level goal to play in the NBA. The top-level goal is then broken down in to subgoals that define characteristics or attributes of an NBA player. Notice that the characteristics and attributes are the types of things that can be developed or controlled: jump shot, handles, be physically fit (be fast, jump high), nutrition, and mental health. These subgoals and characteristics are then broken down into sets of behaviors that promote their development. Jump shot is made up of having great form, making five hundred shots per day, and starting in close.

Handles includes the behaviors of two-ball dribble and between-the-legs dribble. Running fast is made up of run sprints and strong core. Nutrition includes drinking water (avoiding soda), eating protein, and eating vegetables. And finally, mental health includes growth Mindset and staying positive, which includes meditating and "I Am."

Clearly, this sample IG2 Tree is not even close to being complete for reaching the goal of playing professional basketball. In fact, this sample is just a scratch of the surface. However, it should give you an idea of how to build your own IG2 Tree to support your goals. I imagine that a more complete tree for this type of goal might have one hundred or more boxes of subgoals, characteristics, behaviors, and even microbehaviors should you take it that far. A microbehavior is a small part of a larger behavior—for example, the snap of the wrist on the follow-through of a jump shot. Check out the details shown in Figure 5.2.

Important Note: The IG2 Tree that you create for yourself does not have to be limited to only the things you should be doing that support your goals. Your tree can also include the things that you should avoid doing and that distract you from your goal. Not coincidentally, distractions are the topic of our next chapter.

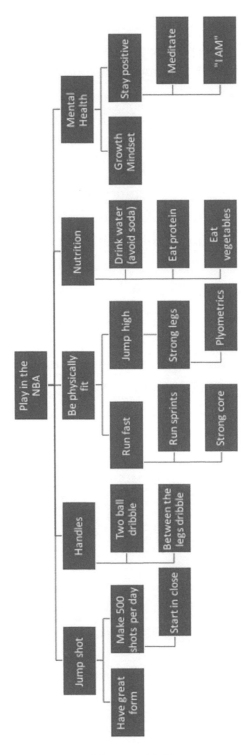

Figure 5.2. A sample IG2 Tree for defining goals and characteristics that support them.

Grit should become more than a word to you. It should become a part of who you are. Defining your IG2 Tree and having a deeper understanding of what it takes to reach your goals is the first step in being able to develop grit. This is part of your engineering pillar. Taking your knowledge and creating a step-by-step plan is the first step in the engineering of your life. Early on in the book you were introduced to the concept of E3. Educate, engineer and empower. To this point we have been doing a lot of educating. Now its time to learn the engineering. More specifically it is time to learn how to build your own plan for success so that you can feel empowered to keep striving. By having your plan laid out, defined, and clearly visible, you can then begin to exhibit the consistent, goal-oriented behaviors that let others see your passion, perseverance, and dedication—so much so that they look at you and say, "That kid has grit."

CHAPTER 6
Social and Digital Distraction

YOU SET A well-defined, clearly stated, and achievable goal. You have outlined the steps you need to accomplish your goal. You know all the behaviors that support reaching your goal. At this point, you might think you have all that you need to start grinding your way toward ultimate success. There is one more bit of preplanning that can be beneficial to the long-term grind: identification of the distractions you will face along the way.

Very few things in life occur without outside influence, especially in today's world where digital transformation has taken over our lives.

This chapter is very simple but very powerful. In this chapter, we are going to define many of the things, both good and bad, that can be a distraction toward the things that you want to accomplish.

Distractions will come in several forms. There are bad distractions and there are good distractions. Either way, they are distractions.

Bad distractions are those things that are not only distracting to your end goals, but also harmful to your mind or body. Bad distractions are most commonly offered up in the form of peer pressure, which makes them extremely powerful. Your teenage years are heavily influenced by the interactions you have with those around you. Use this information as an opportunity to identify the negative impact these things can have on your goals.

Read through the following list of bad distractions. Use the space at the end to add your own ideas of bad distractions.

Bad Distractions (in no particular order)

- Social Media: Social media is a very powerful distractor. The ease with which we have access makes it perhaps the most common distractor. Although social media can certainly be used to find or generate inspiration, you must be careful with the amount of time spent randomly scrolling through nonsense videos. We can't discount that there are social media accounts that can provide valuable information, inspiration, shared stories of success, and more. However, there are many more accounts with less productive content. As a teenager, it is compelling to want to communicate, express opinions, or be entertained. There is certainly a time for that, but the key is to limit the time spent doing so and to be mindful of the things you post. There are too many stories of young athletes who lose opportunities because of a single moment in which they post something that can never be taken back.

It's okay to participate in social media, but do it in a manner that is responsible and limited. And the next time you are on Instagram, follow us at @beast_thinking, @beast_athletics, and @527hoops.

- Video Games: As of the writing of this book, the most popular video game distractions are likely to be *NBA2K* and *Fortnite*, with the latter being the latest craze. As a dad of two sons, I know it is unrealistic to think that kids are going to forego video games entirely. It's therefore unrealistic to even suggest it. The key here for those that do play is limits. Limit the time you spend on video games. When you sit down to play, you should know exactly when you are going to stop. Perhaps play thirty minutes or even sixty minutes, but if four hours later you are still playing, there is certainly an issue with limits. If you find yourself obsessing over a game, constantly discussing a game, and watching hours of videos on a game, then there is certainly an issue with limits.

- Drugs and Alcohol: As I sat to write this section, a part of me thought that this should be a no-brainer. I won't get too deep into the subject because there are entire books on the matter, but drugs and alcohol are a surefire way to close the pathway to any goal. As a teenage athlete, your body needs all the positive energy it can get to support optimal and maximum growth. If drugs and alcohol are an issue for you, then reach out to someone who can help you immediately: a parent, a teacher, a coach, or anyone with whom you are comfortable being open and honest. Get your mind right because the mind controls the brain, and the brain controls the body.

- Sex: Much like the topic above, the conversations you have regarding sex and sexuality should be had with your parents or someone you are close to who can provide you sound advice. During your teen years, your body undergoes changes physically and chemically that have a tremendous impact on your mind and decision making. The desire to feel wanted, loved, desired, admired, or accepted is a very strong force. These feelings should not be tackled alone or without the help of someone who has been through the same thing. Don't rely on friends to guide you through one of the most critical times of your life because they are most likely sharing that same journey. Ultimately, remember that your will, your determination, and your control of your mind can be stronger than anything you will experience.

Use the spaces below to add your ideas of bad distractions.

- _____

- _____

- _____

The term "good distractions" is a play on words. There is no such thing as a good distraction. Good distractions are those things that distract you from your goal but don't cause bodily harm. Notice, however, that I mention *bodily* harm. Good distractions can have a severe impact on your mind. Read through the list of good distractions. Use the space at the end to add your own ideas of good distractions.

Good Distractions (in no particular order):

- Rankings: Over the last decade, as youth sports has exploded into a multi-billion-dollar industry, the concept of rankings has become an annoyingly all-too-common distraction for athletes, parents, and coaches. Rankings are a distraction in that they can allow a highly ranked athlete to develop complacency or an unranked athlete to develop frustration. Thankfully, as a BEAST athlete, you know better than to let rankings impact you in any way. Rankings are never based on a young athlete's mindset, work ethic, grit, or passion, and they are rarely if ever created by individuals with growth mindset.

- Accolades: It's a fantastic accomplishment to achieve, and if that achievement comes with a trophy, an acknowledgment, or some other form of reward, it certainly makes you feel good. I don't want to suggest that receiving an accolade is in and of itself a distraction, but focusing too much on them is definitely a distraction. Accolades can be a great tool for measuring your progress as an athlete. Just be careful to not let accolades overtake your intrinsic motivation to succeed.

- Too Much Praise/Success: A BEAST athlete knows how to use criticism, feedback, and failure to become even better. But similarly, a BEAST athlete knows how to accept praise and success without letting it become a good distraction. Today's digital and hyperconnected world allow us to follow young athletes from anywhere in the world. This brings attention and praise from thousands, hundreds of thousands, or even millions of people, which can turn a hungry BEAST athlete into a complacent one. As you start to excel and people notice, be thankful and humble, but most important, be prepared to keep working word to show them you can be even better.

Use the spaces below to add some of your own ideas of good distractions.

- _____

- _____

- _____

CHAPTER 7

Mindfulness, Meditation, and the Power of "I Am"

CONGRATULATIONS! YOU HAVE made it to what will be the most difficult part of the book. Now is the time to learn how to take control of your own thinking and be the master of your mind. There is no doubt that learning the information in this book is a huge step in the right direction toward achieving your goals. However, it is putting all this information into practice that will create the results that you want. You need to become the engineer, the architect, or even the mad scientist of your life. You can certainly go back and reread parts of the book for better understanding, and you can continue your mindset education by reading the books we have referenced. However, the information in this chapter is what you must learn to build into your everyday life. These techniques, methods, and behaviors are the execution of all the concepts you have learned.

MINDFULNESS

The success you have in translating concepts to practice begins with understanding the basic concept of mindfulness. A quick internet search reveals the Wikipedia definition of mindfulness.

> Mindfulness is the process of bringing one's attention to experiences occurring in the present moment, which one can develop through the practice of meditation and through other training.

Based on this definition, and based on the methods of most meditation practices, the word *mindful* doesn't mean "full mind." In fact, mindfulness is more about focus and attention on fewer things, if not a single thing. Being mindful is achieved through forced awareness of thoughts, or the lack thereof. Being mindful is achieved by being purposefully conscious. By intentionally filling your mind with a single thought, like you would intentionally fill a glass with water, you are being mindful.

The practice of being mindful, or purposely filling your mind, seems like a simple concept or task. The reality is that mindfulness is an immensely challenging task. In large part, the difficulty of being mindful or reaching a state of true mindfulness comes from the way our lives operate outside of the times when we try to be self-aware and focused on our minds. For most adults, teens, and even young kids, our lives are filled with many different people, events, and

@beast_thinking_

activities. This overwhelming amount of stimuli creates an intense amount of mind/brain activity that is difficult to shut off. Pause for a moment and think about your typical day. How many people do you interact with on a given day? How many other students, athletes, teachers, parents, coaches, siblings, and neighbors? How many different subjects do you think about? How many different aspects of your sport or hobby are there that you think about? How many additional activities outside of your typical school day and sports training occur? I bet that if you listed all of these things and their ancillary effects, you would have a very long list. These are all the things that make it difficult to bring your mind to a state where focus is shifted to only one thing. It's like trying to stop a hundred-mile-per-hour fastball from using your face, except being mindful definitely won't leave you with a concussion.

But here is the good news. Like anything else in life, you can learn to become very good at being mindful through consistent, deliberate practice. The consistent, deliberate practice of being mindful is known as meditation. Meditation comes in different forms and means different things to different people.

MEDITATION

If you have heard the word meditation quite a bit lately but are not really sure what it means you are certainly not alone. According the Merriam-Webster dictionary meditation is defined as the act or process of meditating. Don't you hate definitions of words that use a derivative of the same word you want defined? Me too. So lets dig a step deeper. Merriam-Webster defines meditating as

1. To engage in contemplation or reflection
2. To engage in mental exercise (such as concentration on one's breathing or repetition of a mantra) for the purpose of reaching a heightened level of spiritual awareness.

Those seem like some pretty deep definitions. A more simple way to define meditation can be found from the web site www.headspace.com which makes a popular meditation app.

"Meditation isn't about becoming a different person, a new person, or even a better person. It's about training in awareness and getting a healthy sense of perspective. You're not trying to turn off your thoughts or feelings. You're learning to observe them without judgment. And eventually, you may start to better understand them as well." - Headspace

Although the relationship between mindfulness and meditation is very strong, it does not mean that they are the same thing. Mindfulness is a state of being, whereas meditation is an action. meditation is a means of achieving mindfulness. When most people think of meditation, they think of monks sitting perfectly still, cross-legged and with eyes closed. This is certainly an accurate portrayal of the history of meditation because it has been practiced for hundreds of years. But the monk life is no longer dominating the practice of meditation. Meditation has made great strides to becoming mainstream. Recent studies have found meditation to be beneficial in reducing stress, anxiety, depression, and pain. Meditation and mindfulness are becoming mainstream. Athletes and students are no exception when it comes to receiving the benefits of meditation. Today's teenage population are more exposed to stress and anxiety than any generation before them. Meditation is a critical skill that can be used to help teens successfully navigate these important years of their life.

Meditation helps us become mindful.

Given that mindfulness is the reduction of the mind's activity to a single entity, one might argue that it's really mind-less-ness instead of mind-full-ness. The less we think about at a given time, the more mindful we become. What? Less is more? How can less be more? In the process of being mindful, we fill our minds with more of a single thought and less random thinking. Think of filling a glass with liquid. If you fill a glass with eight different colored liquids at the same time, you end up with one full glass of murky, dark liquid. If you fill the same glass with only water, you still end up with a full glass, but it is only one highly concentrated, crystal-clear liquid. Being mindful is filling your mind with one highly concentrated, crystal-clear thought.

Meditation can be done in different ways. The best way is the one that allows you to do it most often. There might certainly be better ways of doing something, but remember that the key to becoming mindful is being consistent and deliberate in your practice of meditation. Meditation can be done passively or actively. In either case, there is still a single, intentional focus.

Passive meditation is the practice of bringing the body

to rest and bringing the mind to focus on a single thought. Most meditation practices will have you focus solely on your breathing. Breathing becomes the one and only focus of the mind. In this type of meditation, you clear your mind of all else. Attention is brought to your inhale and exhale. It's so simple but so difficult. Lifting your maximum weight on the bench press requires 100 percent effort 100 percent of the time during the lift, and this type of meditation requires 100 percent focus 100 percent of the time. Our minds have tendencies to wander. This doesn't happen in minutes or even seconds; it happens in milliseconds if we don't maintain focus.

The key to meditation is in understanding how your mind and body work. There is not a single, particular way to meditate that ensures success for every individual. Meditation works when you can achieve focus regardless of what the method is. For some people, meditation requires a dark and quiet space; others might prefer hearing the sounds of the surrounding environment or even music. Meditation works when you understand the benefits, understand the goal, and practice it. There are tremendous benefits to be had from even just a few minutes of meditation each day.

Here are a few tips to becoming successful at meditation.

1. Be consistent in your practice. Just like stretching, weight lifting, running, or studying, meditation takes time to master. Don't give up if you struggle in the beginning. As you improve, the benefits will be worth the effort.

@beast_thinking_

2. Start with just a few minutes and work your way up to longer periods of time. If you are like most people, you are going to find that maintaining focus is not easy. Start small, build success for a few minutes, and then work your way up to longer periods of time.

3. Find a single idea, thought, or action you can easily focus on. Most guided meditations will suggest you focus on your breath. Inhale. Exhale. For some, this can be very boring and therefore exponentially more difficult to maintain focus on. Focus does not have to be reserved for the breath. Focus on a body part. Then move your focus through the body, paying attention to any feelings or sensations. As you learn more about how your body works (i.e., blood flow, protein synthesis, healing, neurons firing), you can turn your attention to those specific bodily functions.

4. Don't be discouraged if you can't maintain focus. Bring yourself back to focus and continue. Meditation is hard. Nothing worth doing is ever easy.

5. Don't be afraid to personalize your practice. If you find that your focus and mindfulness is helped by listening to sounds or music, then add them to your practice. If you find that staring at a spot on the wall or ceiling keeps your focus better than closing your eyes, then stare at the spot. Meditation is becoming common, but it doesn't mean that your style can't fit you.

Reader Note: If you need help with your practice of meditation, you can find it on your smartphone. From downloadable apps like Calm, Simple Habit, 10% Happier, and Headspace to hardware devices like Muse, you can find tools that will support your goal of becoming better at mindfulness and meditation. These apps and devices are certainly not required for performing meditation, but they do offer the benefit of guidance, tracking, and feedback to help you get a better understanding of your progress in becoming mindful. The Muse device, available from choosemuse. com, tracks brain activity and converts it into sounds. The immediate feedback from the device helps the user maintain or regain focus as the sounds vary.

THE POWER OF "I AM"

Have you ever been in a position where you or someone you know is able to manipulate a situation to achieve a specific outcome? Let's say that you would like a new pair of athletic training shoes, so you ask your parents if you can get them. Your parents simply say no. But rather than taking no for an answer, you proceed to explain to your parents how those shoes are critical to your success. You explain that the bottoms are wider, which gives you a better center of gravity for when you are squatting or lunging during conditioning drills. You might tell them that narrower shoes, like the ones you have, are better for distance running, but when performing plyometrics, they don't provide good stability and therefore increase the chances that you turn an ankle or injure your knee. After a few minutes of sharing this information, your parents change their minds and buy you the shoes.

The chances of your success in this scenario are predicated on two things: (1) that you know legitimate facts of a shoe's purpose (knowledge), and (2) the strength with which you tell your parents that which you know (action confidence). Your knowledge and your confidence have allowed you to change your parents' behavior to fit your own needs and wants. This is often referred to as social engineering.

Social engineering is the ability to manipulate your social environment to your benefit. Learning the skills of social engineering can be very beneficial and are essential for anyone who is a sales professional. In the same way that you can manipulate the environment around you to achieve what you want, you can manipulate your brain into believing. This is brain engineering. This is where you learn the power of "I am."

In the story earlier, the key to success was in the knowledge and the action confidence. Knowing how to act and the willingness to act are critical factors in just about anything you will do in your life, whether it is sports, academics, relationships, or work. Knowledge and confidence.

Knowledge.
Confidence.

Which of these two do you think are more difficult? Don't turn the page until you come up with an answer.

If you answered *confidence*, you are correct. In today's information marketplace, the ability to learn something new is easy. You can pretty much learn anything using the internet, textbooks, audiobooks, TED Talks, YouTube videos, blogs, vlogs, whitepapers, Tweets, Instagram posts, or Snapchats. The compilation of information you consume and retain is what makes up your mental and intellectual capacity, but how you use that information will be determined by your ability to believe strongly that you can succeed and then act upon it. Achieving goals requires identifying the goals, learning how to reach them, believing you can reach them, and behaving like you can reach them. This process involves convincing the brain you are capable. As we saw back in chapter 2, the brain is very capable of sabotaging success. It can be your most powerful ally, or it can be your worst enemy.

One of the most powerful ways of convincing the brain is using the words "I am." In the same way the brain builds myelin to support the idea of muscle memory, the brain can become convinced of a reality through repetition and intention. This new perception then manifests itself in physical form through sports, education, work, relationships, or whatever aspect of your life you are trying to manipulate. Using "I am" affirmations is a way of driving conscious positivity from the mind to the brain to the body. The concepts and ideas behind conscious positivity have been found to heal critically injured people, pull people from the depths of depression, help athletes overcome obstacles, and so much more.

"I am" affirmations are the opposite of meditation in that they are very easy. They are also not mutually exclusive from meditation as they can be used as a form of meditation. "I am" statements can be short and sweet or they can be longer complete thoughts and actions. As a young athlete I expect that creating a few short and direct affirmations is a better place to start. Let's take a stab at starting a list of "I am" affirmations.

Tips for creating your "I Am" statements:

- Start with four to five statements and work your way up to ten to twelve.
- Keep your statements short. As time goes by, you might find the need to expand upon an affirmation and provide more detail, but start with simple statements.
- Intermix "I am" statements that are currently true with those that you want to become part of your reality. For example, maybe you are a very fast athlete, but you have a goal of being more agile. Even though you are already fast, include "I am fast" as one of your affirmations along with "I am agile."
- Only use statements for which your behaviors support achieving success. You can't include "I am a great shooter" in your list of affirmations but not take the actions to actually be a great shooter. The affirmations are not voodoo magic that create realities from nothing. Affirmations are a powerful mind hack that makes behaviors that much more effective in reaching your goals. Affirmations train the brain to command the body to act confidently based upon an existing knowledge base.
- Repeat your affirmations every day, twice a day, three times a day, or more! You can also record your affirmations as they grow in number and complexity.

Try to say or listen to your "I am" statements soon after you wake up, just before bed, and at any other time throughout the day where you have a few moments. The more consistent you are, the more convincing they become.

Your "I am" statements are flexible. You can modify, remove and add new statements at any time.

A great way to help bring your "I am" statements to life is by creating a vision board. This allows the brain to consume your conscious positivity through sight in addition to sound. A vision board is a visual representation of your "I am" statements. It can contain pictures, drawings, words, sayings, or anything else that can convey the success you are trying to create. If you are working toward becoming a faster athlete, you might have a picture of Usain Bolt on your vision board. If you are working on becoming a better basketball player, you might have a picture of Kobe Bryant or Steph Curry on your vision board. Use images that represent your goals and achievements.

To create a vision board, start by writing down your goals and subgoals. Then think of all the characteristics and traits that are required to reach those goals. Sound familiar? It should, because we explored this very same process in chapter 5. If you started the process of developing your inverted goals and grit tree, then you are well on your way to having the foundation of your vision board.

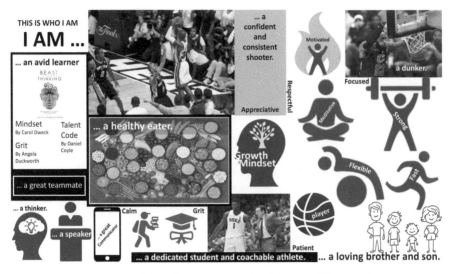

Figure 7.1. A vision board turns the ideas of "I am" into a visual representation of who you are and what you want.

Just like your "I am" statements, your vision board is not a static creation. You can, and should, constantly revisit your vision board to replace, remove, or add new images.

CHAPTER 8
Cognitive Conditioning and Stress Training

FOR AS LONG as I can remember the ideas, philosophies and strategies for improving athletic performance has focused on physical development. This over emphasis on physical development left many athletes with a huge void when comparing athletic performance in controlled and static conditions versus the chaotic and dynamic conditions of an athletic competition. Recently, however, a small group of practitioners, educators and researchers have begun to bring to light the significant impact of training the brain. Like your biceps, quads, hamstrings, pectorals, and calves, the brain is a muscle that can, and must be trained in order to maximize your evolution as an athlete. This chapter is going to focus on stress training in two forms.

Since the brain is a muscle it must be stressed in order to grow. This chapter will teach you new forms of training that will improve the performance of your brain as it relates to your sport specific skills and movements. The second form of stress training is learning to manage and control stress imposed by real time in-game situations.

Back in Chapter 2: Brain vs Mind we began with an analogy of a race car and its driver. The car being representative of the physical and the driver being the mind. Now think of the entire car as the brain and the body. Focusing on an athlete's physical strength and conditioning while not including cognitive conditioning in a training regimen is the equivalent of adding more horsepower to a race car that is driven by an untrained driver. You can't expect success to be anything but incrementally better, if at all, if the driver isn't equipped with the cognitive abilities to handle the speed, power and agility of the race car.

Investing thousands of dollars and hundreds of hours into strength, conditioning and sports specific training without an element of cognitive conditioning will not result in maximal outcomes. Over the years of working with hundreds of athletes from novices to professionals I have seen time and time again how work in the gym fails to translate into in-game success. The disconnect stems from the inability for the athlete to operate in an environment with exponentially more variables than the training scenarios.

Sports performance is dependent on three areas: 1) physical preparedness, 2) tactical mastery of sports specific skills and 3) cognitive conditioning. Researchers are just now scratching the surface on the cognitive conditioning impacts on sports performance. It's not difficult to see that most of today's top athletes are highly skilled and physical conditioned to perform at peak levels. What we often don't see are cognitive and psychological skills that allow them to better leverage the physical capabilities and manage stressful situations.

So, what is cognitive conditioning?

Let's start by defining the word cognitive. Merriam Webster defines cognitive as "relating to, being, or involving conscious intellectual activity."

The American Psychological Association defines cognitive conditioning as "a process in which a stimulus is repeatedly paired with an imagined or anticipated response or behavior."

Since you are a young athlete and not a clinical researcher you are probably more interested in a definition that you can relate to. Cognitive conditioning is training the brain and mind to give athletes control of conscious reactions to external events. Cognitive conditioning trains the decision-making part of the brain to process external stimuli with the goal of efficiently and effectively completing a motor function. Overtime this teaches the brain how to properly regulate brainwave activity and emotions under various degrees of stress. When you train to improve muscular strength, you do so by applying stress to the muscular system. Dumbbell curls build bigger biceps, push-ups build chest and shoulder muscles, pull-ups build back muscles, and yoga stresses the body to create better flexibility and mobility. These are all common exercises that people do in order to create physical change in their bodies. Cognitive conditioning is brain stress training to create change in the brain. Brain stress training can be used to improve:

- Hand-eye coordination
- Selective attention
- Mental focus
- Working memory
- High speed decision making
- Vision
- Impulse control
- Mindset management
- Mental physicality

As a human, stress will forever be part of your daily life. As an athlete, student, child, sibling, co-worker, spouse, parent, etc. stress will come in many forms and in varying degrees. Sports in and of themselves do not exist without the existence of a stress stimulus. Where would the excitement come from if there wasn't a designed system for preventing success every time? How rewarding would it be to win if there wasn't a chance of losing? The thrill of victory is on a thrill because of the agony of defeat. The thrill of victory is rooted in the ability to overcome the stress stimulus of intense competition, both externally from opponents and internally from one's own mind and body. From slow paced sports like golf to the high paced sports like soccer and basketball to the intermittent action sports like football, baseball, softball and volleyball, stressors are everywhere. Golfers are playing against a course built to stress the athlete and deter success. Basketball, volleyball and soccer have fast moving constant defenders' intent on stressing and preventing success. Athletes in these sports are exposed to a constant and dynamic set of stimuli that are aimed at preventing success. Athletes in basketball, volleyball, soccer, baseball, etc are not afforded extended periods of time for handling stress and making decisions in sport. They don't have time to stop and think. Decisions have to be made fast, emotions have to be controlled, and thoughts have to be owned in order to give the best chance at favorable outcomes.

Stress.
Stress.
Stress.
Stress.

The word stress can be used as a noun or a verb as in the two sentences below.

1. Heavier weights apply more stress on your muscles.
2. Hudson was severely stressed shooting the game winning free throws.

It is important to know that there are not only different definitions and uses of the word stress but that there are different types of stress too. Stresses that are beneficial to the brain and body, those that bring about positive change, are called eustress. On the other side of the coin are the stresses that have detrimental or negative effects on the body. These negative stresses are called distress. We are going to focus on creating opportunities for using eustress to make you a better human, but at the same time we will also teach you some tips and tricks for dealing with distress.

This chapter is intentional in its merger of the concepts of cognitive conditioning and stress management because the two are not mutually exclusive, in fact, they are very tightly aligned. The goal of every athlete, when it comes to stress, is to be able to rely on cognitive conditioning practices to provide highly developed and rapid reaction time with tightly controlled emotional response to stress.

Our bodies are built to be able to handle stress, and even adapt to it, but only to a certain point. We are not built for prolonged periods of stress and therefore whenever we experience any type of stress we must have time to be able to recover.

Stress + Rest = Growth
Stress + Stress = Injury

The human body reacts differently to eustress and distress. The brain determines which chemicals are released and produced based on the interpretation of the stressor. When the brain perceives a potential stressor as a challenge it secretes a higher level of a hormone called DHEA (Dehydroepiandrosterone). However, when a stressor is perceived as a threat to your safety the body initiates the fight, flight or freeze (F^3) response and secretes increased levels of cortisol and adrenaline. As you might assume from the terms, fight refers to the body's natural reaction to aggressively confront a stimulus, flight is the body's natural reaction to run from or avoid a stimulus, and freeze is the body's natural reaction to lock up and prevent normal function.

When you are challenged to a race, a competitive drill, a new personal best, etc. the brain perceives this as a challenge, not as a threat to your safety. In this case, the psychological stress of the challenge is helping your brain grow. DHEA is a neurosteroid that helps your brain much the same way steroids help your muscles. For several hours after a stress response the brain rewires itself to learn from the experience. This rewiring, or learning, then helps you the next time you are presented with a similar challenge. The most common response to this stressor would be fight. Not that you are going to fight the person delivering the challenge, but that you will confront the challenge.

On the other hand, if you are taking a jog through a scenic mountain trail and a bear appears, the brain does not record this as a challenge. In this case, higher levels of cortisol and adrenaline are produced by the body rather than DHEA. In this example the response is not as easy to predict. One would assume that flight or freeze would be much more common responses than fighting a bear.

One of the keys to brain stress training, cognitive conditioning, is to teach you how to handle stress. As alluded to earlier, your perception of stress is a key indicator of your ability to thrive and grow in a given situation. You can train your brain to be good at stress. This doesn't mean that you won't ever be stressed by a situation. It means that you will know how to control the responses you have to external stimuli that create the stressed situation. The first and perhaps biggest factor in your ability to grow from stress is your mindset. Think for a moment about the training that elite athletes might endure; weight training, skills training, film study, etc. Now contrast that with the training that an elite military unit might endure; underwater submersion, firearms training, psychological duress, parachuting, etc. Whether we are talking about the athlete or the military unit the experience of undergoing stress allows the brain to develop a stronger stress inoculation. It's like giving your brain a flu shot for stress. By stressing the brain in a controlled purposeful manner, it becomes better prepared when stress is induced in the chaos of athletic play or military combat.

You have to have a positive mindset toward stress. As we noted in the earlier chapter on mindsets, you have to embrace and seek out challenges that often create stressful situations. In addition, you have to be able to perform controlled mindfulness and breathing in order to prevent the body's natural fight, flight or freeze from occurring. Earlier in this chapter we defined the F3 responses for perceived threat. The key here is the perceived threat. In the example of the bear, that is an actual threat. Athletics, however, are high stress environments where untrained athletes can perceive non-life-threatening situations to be just as severe. An athlete called upon to perform in the waning seconds of a must win game cannot afford to allow the natural response of flight or freeze. Either of these responses would result in a significant decline in performance. Athletes need to be able to control the stress response to ensure that they can remain in control and perform at the highest level.

No matter what sport you pick there are elements of the sport that are designed to decrease your chances of success. Whether it be human elements like defenders, or natural elements like a bunker these deterrents are part of the challenge of sport. For sports that move in multiple dimensions at high speeds it would only make sense to train in a similar fashion. The problem however is that many trainers and athletes neglect to add cognitive elements to their training.

Many, if not all, trainers will agree that agility is the ability to move easily and quickly through space. A common technique for teaching agility is to use static cones set up that require an athlete to run around, by or change direction at each cone as shown in Figure 8.1. No doubt doing exercises such as this can improve agility. The problem, however, is that unlike these cones, sports happen in a more dynamic manner.

Figure 8.1. A simple agility drill for change of direction against a static stimulus.

@beast_thinking_

In the exercise the cones are not moving; they are static entities. The athlete can fully anticipate the arrival at the cone. Sports competitions on the other hand don't have defenses that just stand in one spot and allow athletes to move about freely. While the cone drill helps an athlete master the biomechanics of stop and go, change of direction, and/or change of speed, it doesn't provide any cognitive training that allows for development of reaction time.

Cognitive conditioning adds dynamic elements to training that merges biomechanics with mental elements to provide more accurate reflections of the in-game experience. Figure 8.2 shows an athlete working with a set of three lights (www.fitlighttraining.com) that flash randomly. Like the cones the athlete must perform a behavior upon the flash; run to it, run away, jump, etc. The significant difference here is that, unlike the cones, the athlete doesn't know which light will flash and therefore must read and react. A static read and react (cones) versus dynamic read and react (lights) is the simple, but impactful, difference of adding a stressor to the brain.

Figure 8.2. A read and react agility drill using dynamic light stimulus to help improve cognitive ability and agility.

By designing and performing cognitive conditioning drills that introduce stress for the brain and the body athletes can better mimic the in-game experience. If you don't have access to dynamic light systems like the FitLights system you can create similar experiences using easy to find components. Figure 8.3 shows an athlete working with 5 colored, numbered dots (sklz.implus.com/) laid out on the floor. The dots themselves are a static stimulus. To add a dynamic cognitive element to the dots a trainer or second athlete would randomly call out a number or color. The athlete performing the exercise would then react. A random number generator can be used to ensure the athlete does not begin to memorize the pattern allowing them to make pre-determined movements as opposed to true reaction-based movements.

Figure 8.3. A read and react agility drill using colored
and numbered dots with randomized call outs.

Additional modifications can be made to the dots exercise
that increase difficulty and/or change the cognitive skill being
trained. For example, rather than calling out a single number
or color the trainer can call out five or six colors or numbers at
a time. The athlete must then engage their short-term working
memory with the biomechanics of the movement pattern.
Additionally, the trainer can intermix colors and numbers.
Table 8.1 shows a sample workout. There are six configurations
of numbers, colors and both numbers and colors. Athletes
can perform the exercises for a defined period of time for
maximum number of called items or athletes can perform a
certain number of items for minimum time. You should use a
time that has value for the sport you play, not to exceed 30s,
giving maximum effort for each interval.

	Numbers		Colors			Colors And Numbers			Number Blocks of 5			Color Blocks of 5			Color/Number Blocks of 5		
1	3	2	Red	Green	Yellow	1	3	3	3	4	4	Green	Red	Orange	Green	2	4
2	4	4	Green	Red	Orange	4	4	5	3	2	1	Blue	Green	Green	3	Red	2
4	1	1	Red	Blue	Green	3	2	2	2	3	2	Orange	Green	Red	2	5	Green
5	2	5	Green	Red	Red	2	2	2	3	5	4	Blue	Blue	Red	Yellow	Blue	5
3	3	4	Yellow	Yellow	Blue	5	4	3	5	1	3	Orange	Yellow	Red	2	3	Green
4	2	1	Red	Green	Blue	3	2	2	2	5	3	Orange	Green	Orange	5	Orange	Blue
2	3	5	Red	Green	Red	5	2	2	2	1	2	Orange	Yellow	Red	Yellow	Orange	5
2	3	5	Green	Yellow	Yellow	2	1	2	3	5	1	Orange	Yellow	Blue	Blue	4	3
5	2	5	Yellow	Red	Orange	3	2	3	4	3	3	Orange	Blue	Yellow	4	Green	Yellow
1	2	5	Yellow	Blue	Green	3	2	3	1	5	2	Red	Orange	Green	Orange	4	1
2	3	4	Orange	Orange	Blue	5	3	1	1	2	5	Yellow	Green	Green	3	4	5
5	5	4	Yellow	Blue	Blue	4	3	3	5	2	4	Green	Orange	Yellow	Red	Red	5
5	3	5	Blue	Yellow	Blue	5	3	5	3	3	3	Green	Orange	Yellow	Orange	1	Blue
4	4	2	Yellow	Orange	Red	5	1	5	2	1	2	Blue	Red	Red	3	3	4
5	1	1	Orange	Orange	Orange	2	2	2	1	5	1	Yellow	Blue	Red	2	Green	Yellow
4	1	1	Red	Yellow	Red	3	4	5	3	1	4	Green	Blue	Blue	Green	5	3
2	5	4	Red	Green	Yellow	4	2	5	3	2	1	Green	Green	Blue	3	Orange	Orange
1	1	1	Red	Red	Green	2	2	1	1	1	2	Yellow	Green	Red	5	1	3
4	2	1	Red	Yellow	Blue	5	5	3	1	3	1	Orange	Blue	Blue	Blue	5	Blue
5	1	3	Green	Blue	Yellow	1	1	1	5	2	4	Orange	Yellow	Orange	Blue	3	5

Table 8.1. A sample table for using colors and numbers to build a read and react cognitive conditioning agility drill.

Introducing cognitive conditioning elements to athletic training is not limited to just movements and reactions. Sport specific training with the same principles can amplify the effectiveness of skills training. Combining cognitive conditioning with skills training teaches the brain an association between the cognitive skill and the sports related skill. In figure 8.4 the FitLight drill shown earlier is modified to include a basketball ball handling element. As before the athlete must react at the sight of a light but now the reaction includes a specific dribble move:

- Red light – crossover dribble
- Green light – between the legs
- Blue light – behind the back

Figure 8.4. Using dynamic light sequences with ball handling is an example of combining cognitive conditioning with sport specific training.

This similar setup can be used to duplicate sport-specific movements for baseball, volleyball, football, soccer and more.

All it takes is some creativity and it is easy to find new, fun and effective ways to challenge yourself during your training sessions.

Be sure to follow @BEAST_THINKING_ on Instagram to see some of the cognitive conditioning drills used on our athletes.

Have you ever heard someone say one of the following?

- You can learn from failure.
- You need to embrace failure.
- Don't be afraid to fail.
- Fail fast to move forward.
- Overcoming failure is the key to success.

I am 100% sure you have heard or read something similar to the above statements because we specifically discussed this earlier in the book. It is important to understand that in order for those statements to be true the failure in question has to be calculated in nature. This means that what you are failing at is actually achievable within the limits of the laws of physics and your genetic ceiling. Constant failure at seemingly unattainable goals will deter anyone from continuing to work. Overcoming failure must be combined with intermittent, even if limited, amounts of success. For example, if an 11 year old, 4 foot 8 inch basketball player wants to dunk a basketball on a regulation goal there is going to be a tremendous amount of failure. The ability to reach this goal is years ahead of this player. So rather than experiencing constant failure with zero chance of success, the failure should be calculated, coached and combined with instances of success. In this case, perhaps lowering the rim to allow the player to learn the footwork and timing, build muscle, and mentally feel success. Then raising the rim in one half inch increments to challenge the athlete in an-going manner.

As with any type of training the drills and exercises performed should be carefully created to the appropriate level. This does not mean that athlete is not challenged but it does mean that it should not be too hard to perform with some degree of success. This also does not mean that the drills and exercises should be too easy. Any type of training activity needs to be a blend of success and failure, as both are powerful teaching tools. Figure 8.5 shows the effects of proper training difficulty on skill development.

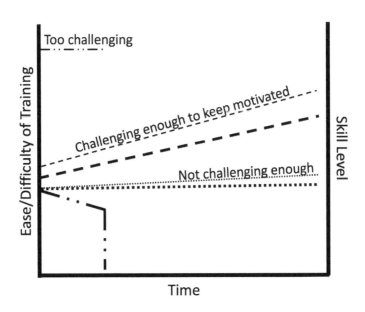

Figure 8.5. A chart that describes the importance of building age and skill appropriate training plans.

Figure 8.5 shows training that is too easy results in very little increase in skill level. On the other hand, training that is too difficult results in an athlete not wanting to train and therefore skill level declines quickly. The most appropriate level of training is that which is challenging enough to keep the athlete motivated to continue. The right level of difficulty allows the athlete to experience both challenge and success. Constantly going outside the comfort zone results in the most significant improvement in skill level.

I have witnessed many coaches use drills far too difficult for an athlete. Take the following examples:

- Basketball coach having beginners practice advanced dribbling moves or shooting from way beyond capable range.
- Baseball/softball coach teaching athletes to hit by throwing high speed pitches.
- Volleyball coach teaching high speed spikes to athletes that can't reach over the net.

If you work with a coach that is not adjusting the training to be appropriate to your level then that coach is doing you a disservice.

The ease/difficulty of training is not limited to just physical development and sports specific skills training. Cognitive conditioning drills must be customized for each athlete. When working with athletes to develop reaction time and working memory each athlete will be different. A more advanced athlete might be able to perform given 6 to 8 pieces of information while another might only perform with 3 or

4. For example, in Table 8.5, the example shows using blocks of 5 (numbers or colors) during a drill. This can be decreased or increased to be more specific to a given athlete.

Don't be fooled or misled by the idea that grit means you are always doing what is most difficult. Grit is to persist, maintain passion, and remain motivated in face of challenges that are relevant to you. Every athlete's journey is different. Every athlete progresses at a different rate.

The challenges presented you during training create stress. Athletic competition, like training creates stress. However, athletic competition isn't just a physical stress. The competitive parts of athletics create physical, mental and emotional stress. Typical athletic training teaches athletes how to handle the physical stresses of competition. But what about the mental and emotional stress?

Training for the mental stress of athletic competition is done by adding cognitive conditioning to your training regimen. As noted earlier, cognitive conditioning enhances mental capabilities that complement physical capabilities. Better all-around performance in competition relies on the brain and the body working together. The right movements in the right space at the right times are what allow athletes to win the small battles throughout a competitive event.

Coaches, parents, trainers, scientists and even athletes themselves are now starting to realize that perhaps the most powerful ally to have in an athletic competition is a positive mindset. Having a positive mindset includes the ability to manage the emotional stress of athletic competition. Have you ever been in a situation where the outcome of a game or match falls squarely on your shoulders? Are you the quarterback that needs to lead a game winning drive for a district title? Are you at the free throw line with only a few seconds left down a point in the state championship? Are you serving for game point in a rivalry game? Are you pitching for the final out of a playoff game?

The outcome of each of these events is a merger between your physical abilities, mental capacity and emotional control. How will you interpret the elevated heart rate, sweaty palms, and knot in your stomach? Is it nervousness? Is it anxiousness? Is it excitement? Have you trained your mind to control your brain to control your body in these situations? If your training has not included physical, mental and emotional challenges it is unlikely that you will understand how to manage them in a critical game situation. This is why it is important that your training be challenging at all three levels. During a challenging training session, you might get emotional at your inability to complete a timed or scored drill. After several attempts you are getting frustrated. This is where you must reset your mind and focus. The mind controls the brain and the brain controls the body. If you let a frustrated mind prevail it will be difficult for the brain to guide the body in a way that creates success. Let's look at a specific scenario.

A basketball player is performing a shooting drill in which they must shoot jump shots from 8 different spots on the floor moving continuously through the 8 spots, show in Figure 8.6. After the 8 spots they must make 2 free throws.

@beast_thinking_

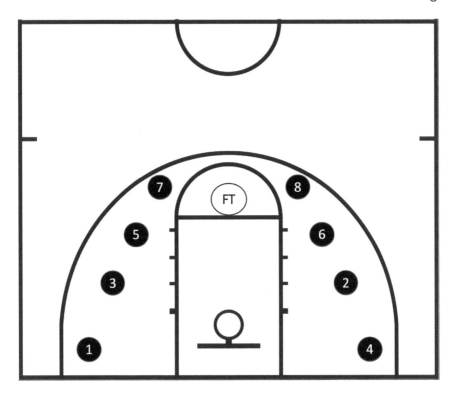

The goal is to make 6 of the 8 shots plus the two free throws. Think of the different physical, mental and emotional challenges that can arise from this drill and how they can map to an athletic competition.

Physical challenges

- Moving from spot to spot
- Getting feet turned and shoulder square
- Shooting with proper balance
- Shooting the basketball with proper form

Mental Challenges

- Remembering the order of the shots
- Staying focused on proper form and mechanics

Emotional Challenges

- Need to make 6 of 8
- Need to make 2 free throws
- What is response after first miss? Second miss? Failed attempt?
- Can the athlete control rising emotions during progression? What does the athlete feel/do when 5 for 7 and needing the last shot? What do they do feel when needing to make final free through to achieve success?

This is just a simple of a basketball drill created to add additional elements. But keep in mind that this is just an example and might need to be adjusted for different athletes. Maybe 4 of 8 with 2 free throws in a more realistic starting point. Maybe 8 for 8 with 2 free throws if you are an advanced player. Or maybe all 8 shots and free throws have to be a perfect swish.

The important part of a drill like this is to learn how to control the feelings and emotions as the pressure mounts toward the end of the drill. Much like a competition scenario where shots have more meaning toward an end result each shot is really just as important as the next but the mind/brain begin to adjust the body's response as the drill progresses into the later shots.

Take a moment and use the space below to create a drill specific to your sport that includes physical, mental and emotional challenges. In addition, make notes on how you can handle these challenges.

Drill Details:

Drill Goal:

Physical Challenges:

-

-

-

-

Mental Challenges:

-

-

-

-

Emotional Challenges:

-

-

-

-

How do you control the emotions of pressure situations? First and foremost, the answer is never to stop thinking about the situation. You can't run or hide from the game winning moment available to you. The process of performing under pressure begins with your understanding that breathing is a powerful tool. In the last chapter we introduced mindfulness, meditation and the power of breathing. Control over your breath provides direct access to control over your response mechanism. In pressure situations you don't want a fight or a flight response. The best athletes in the world train themselves to handle pressure situations. So much so that they are not only able to perform through them but they have learned to thrive in them. Training your mind, brain and body are the only ways to ensure that your athletic capabilities are maximized in a way that is unhindered by your emotional response.

This is why it is very common to find athletes who can perform in an outstanding way in practice or drills but falter when it comes to game situations. Not being able to control your emotional response to pressure situations diminishes that athletic capabilities of even the best. Along the same lines, this is also why mediocre athletes can outperform their physical capabilities. Using the mind to instill confidence and control emotions elevates athletes to the highest levels.

CONCLUSION AND CALL TO ACTION

The end of this book is just the beginning if you are committed to becoming the best version of yourself. Reading this book is an incredibly big first step, but it is no doubt the easiest step. The information you read, as well as the concepts, terms, and skills you have learned in this book, are only as powerful as you allow them to be. The words in the previous pages have to be followed up with deeper thought and action. Lucky for you, we, the authors, didn't just give you words, thoughts, and ideas; we gave you blueprints on how to take action to convert those words, thoughts, and ideas into realities.

Remember the three pillars to creating the changes in your life: education, engineering, and empowerment. This book is the perfect tool for education and engineering. Throughout the pages of the book, you have been educated on the tools, mechanisms, strategies, and science of how humans can create change. Similarly, you have been taught how to engineer your results through goal setting, grit, mindfulness, and more. Now it is time for you to begin with small successes that will empower you to accomplish larger and more rewarding achievements in your life.

Everyone's path to greatness is going to vary. For some of you, it might take reading this book again. For others, there might be a decision to dive even further into the concepts of growth mindset, grit, deep practice, or meditation. Regardless of what your next step might entail, be responsible for the call to action that we present to you as a young student athlete and, more important, as a BEAST Thinker.

The most difficult part of this information will undoubtedly be your ability to find the intrinsic motivation to make it part of your everyday life. The information in this book has been proven to change the course of lives. From athletes to scholars to parents to business executives there is little skepticism about the power of a positive mindset. Yet, despite access to this information there only so few who capitalize on it. This is because of the fact that it all comes back to a person's ability to be consistently motivated to achieve. Find what drives you. Find what moves you. Find your passion. Then educate, engineer and empower your way to all you dream of.

REFERENCES

Here is some follow-up reading list for athletes, students, parents, coaches, teachers, and anyone else who is looking to use one's mind to proactively create change.

Growth Mindset: The New Psychology of Success by Carol Dweck

This is a foundational component to BEAST Thinking. The majority of the book is appropriately written for a teenage reader. Some content will come across as disinteresting or irrelevant for the teenage reader.

Grit by Angela Duckworth

Duckworth addresses the principles set forth in chapter 3 of this book, "Mindset." It provides many examples of the power of passion, persistence, and motivation as keys to success. The majority of the book is appropriately written for a teenage reader. Some content will come across as disinteresting or irrelevant for the teenage reader.

The Talent Code by Daniel Coyle

Doyle writes a fascinating book that explores the specifics of elite sports and arts development, performance, and coaching in areas around the world. The book is appropriate for a teenage reader.

You Are a Badass by Jen Sincero

Sincero details the mindset and actions for taking charge and owning the events in your life. The concepts discussed are deeply rooted in the principles of growth mindset and grit. Some of the content is not appropriate for a teenage reader.